P9-ASN-614

National Defense Research Institute

SOLDIERS

FOR

PEACE

An Operational Typology

Bruce R. Pirnie

William E. Simons

Prepared for the
Office of the Secretary of Defense

RAND

Approved for public release; distribution unlimited

LIBRARY
COLBY-SAWYER COLLEGE
NEW LONDON, NH 03257

JX
1981
.P7
P56
1996
c.1

#34675039

Despite increased interest in peace operations in recent years, the study of peace operations remains a semantic morass, because there is no generally accepted classification of such operations for analysts and decisionmakers. Even fundamental concepts are frequently misunderstood or are interpreted in different ways. This confusion increases the danger that peace operations will become murky and ill-defined, as is often alleged by critics.

This report presents a typology of peace operations developed during "Guidelines for U.S. Involvement in Peace Operations," a project sponsored by the Office of the Assistant Secretary of Defense (Strategy and Requirements). The project was completed in two phases. Results of Phase One are reported in this document, and results of Phase Two are reported in Bruce R. Pirnie and William E. Simons, *Soldiers for Peace: Critical Operational Issues,* RAND, Santa Monica, California, MR-583-OSD, 1996. This typology is intended as a primer for those concerned with peace operations. Properly used, it should promote greater clarity and better-informed decisions.

This research was performed within the International Security and Defense Policy Center of RAND's National Defense Research Institute, a federally funded research and development center sponsored by the Office of the Secretary of Defense, the Joint Staff, and the defense agencies. Comments and inquiries are welcome and should be addressed to the authors.

CONTENTS

Preface iii

Figures ix

Summary xi

Acknowledgments xxiii

Acronyms and Abbreviations xxv

Chapter One
   INTRODUCTION 1
   Purpose of the Study 1
   Study Approach 2
      Quasi-Historical Method 2
      Operational Perspective 3
      Precise Typology Versus Messy Execution 4
   Use of This Typology 5
      Understanding the Limitations 5
      Selecting the Optimal Type of Operation 6
      Evaluating a Peace Operation 6
   Conduct of the Project 7
      Phase One 8
      Phase Two 8
      Information Cutoff 8

Chapter Two
   DEFINING PEACE OPERATIONS 9
   Charter of the United Nations 9
      Chapter VI 9
      Chapter VII 9

Criteria That Bound Peace Operations   11
   Consent of the Parties   12
   Impartiality   13
Issue of Domestic Jurisdiction   14

Chapter Three
SPECTRUM OF PEACE OPERATIONS   17
An Operational Typology   17
Diplomacy   18
Peace Operations   19
   Observation   19
   Interposition   21
   Transition   24
   Security for Humanitarian Aid   30
   Peace Enforcement   33
Enforcement   37
   Korea   37
   Kuwait   37
Overview of an Operational Typology   38
   Diplomacy–Peace Operations–Enforcement   38
   Peace Operations and Their Variants   40
   Historical and Current Peace Operations Classified by
      Type   42

Chapter Four
EVALUATING PEACE OPERATIONS   45
Fulfilling the Mandate   45
Peace-Keeping   46
   Observation   46
   Interposition   49
More-Ambitious Operations   50
   Transition   50
   Security for Humanitarian Aid   55
   Peace Enforcement   57
Summary   61
   Peace-Keeping   62
   More-Ambitious Operations   62

Chapter Five
    CONCLUSIONS.   65
    A Differentiated View.   65
    Fruitful Comparisons   66
    Basis for Reform   67

Appendix
A. TERMS USED IN THIS REPORT   69
B. *AGENDA FOR PEACE*.   75

Bibliography   81

FIGURES

S.1. Peace Operations and Their Variants xvi
3.1. Diplomacy–Peace Operations–Enforcement 39
3.2. Peace Operations and Their Variants 41
3.3. Historical and Current Peace Operations Classified by
      Type 43
4.1. Evaluating Observation Operations 46
4.2. Evaluating Interposition Operations 49
4.3. Evaluating Transition Operations. 51
4.4. Evaluating Security for Humanitarian Aid
      Operations 55
4.5. Evaluating Peace Enforcement Operations 57
B.1. Typology of Peace Operations in *Agenda for
      Peace—1992* 78

The typology of peace operations presented in this report focuses on operational aspects. It should help decisionmakers to understand the limitations of peace operations, to select the optimal type of operation for a given situation, and to evaluate the success of an operation.

LEGAL BASIS OF PEACE OPERATIONS[1]

The Charter of the United Nations describes a system of collective security having two modalities: pacific settlement (Chapter VI) and action with respect to threats to the peace (Chapter VII). Chapter VI lists the traditional techniques of diplomacy, including negotiation, inquiry, mediation, conciliation, arbitration, judicial settlement, resort to regional agencies or arrangements, and other peaceful means. Chapter VII concerns forceful ways of dealing with threats to peace, breaches of peace, and acts of aggression. Article 42 of Chapter VII empowers the Security Council to take action by air, land, and sea forces to maintain or restore international peace and security.

Over the past five decades, the Security Council has developed peace operations, an ad hoc response to conflict not addressed in the Charter. In practice, the Security Council has invoked both Chapter VI and Chapter VII. Invoking Chapter VI has implied that lethal force was authorized in self-defense while accomplishing the mandate.

---

[1]Definitions of terms associated with peace operations are presented in Appendix A.

Invoking Chapter VII has implied that lethal force was authorized to accomplish the mandate, coercing parties if necessary.

CRITERIA THAT BOUND PEACE OPERATIONS

Consent and impartiality are the criteria that bound peace operations.

Consent of the Parties

Consent means that parties to a conflict are willing to help accomplish the mandate. *Parties* are entities that the Security Council believes are responsible for conflict, implying that they control significantly large forces, but not that they have any particular legal status. Parties have included clan leaders (Somalia), self-declared governments (Bosnian Serb authority in Pale), and, of course, member states in the United Nations. To date, no peace operation has been initiated without at least initial consent from the parties.

Impartiality

Impartiality means that the Security Council has decided not to take sides, based on its judgment that all parties share responsibility for a conflict; it identifies neither aggressor nor victim. Not taking sides implies that the Council will not try to attain the political-military aims of any one party to the exclusion of other parties' aims. Parties often insist that all actions of the peace force be neutral in their effect, i.e., affect all parties equally. But even the least intrusive peace operation is highly unlikely to affect all parties equally.

If the Security Council judges that the parties do not share responsibility but, rather, that there is an aggressor who bears all the responsibility, it may authorize a range of actions directed against the aggressor, as in Korea and Kuwait, but peace operations are precluded by definition.

AN OPERATIONAL TYPOLOGY OF PEACE OPERATIONS

Peace operations are highly political, but they should also make operational sense; otherwise, military forces should not be employed. An operational typology looks at peace operations very much as a Force Commander must. With as much precision as the subject allows, this typology defines peace operations in ways that he would find helpful.

Over the past five decades, the Security Council has authorized five types of peace operations: observation, interposition, transition, security for humanitarian aid, and peace enforcement. Observation and interposition together comprise the repertoire of traditional peace-keeping. Transition, security for humanitarian aid, and peace enforcement go beyond traditional peace-keeping and are therefore considered more-ambitious operations. Peace enforcement occurs when the Security Council responds forcefully to recalcitrance during operations conducted under Chapter VII. Each type of operation is described separately below.

Observation

In this type of operation, the peace force is expected to monitor compliance with agreements, international law, or resolutions of the Security Council; report violations; and often mediate resolution of violations among the parties.

There are two subtypes of observation with different implications for decisionmakers. The first subtype is intended to help implement agreement among the parties. There is no implied commitment that the Security Council would respond in any particular way if violations occur. The second subtype is intended to deter. There is an implied commitment that the Security Council or member states acting on its behalf would respond with particular alacrity and severity in the event of violations.

Interposition

The peace force is expected to control a buffer zone between the parties. *Control* implies that the force will detect violations and challenge those responsible for them, not that the force will defend the buffer zone against large-scale incursion. Interposition is more intrusive than observation, because the parties relinquish sovereign rights over the territory within the buffer zone. By relinquishing those rights, the parties allow their forces to disengage, diminishing the likelihood of confrontation, and in some cases the parties gain strategic warning of attack.

There are two subtypes of interposition mandate; each has different implications for decisionmakers. The first subtype is intended to help implement agreement among the parties. There is no implied commitment that the Security Council will respond in any particular way to incursion. The second subtype is intended to deter. There is an implied commitment that the Security Council or member states acting on its behalf would respond with particular alacrity and severity in the event of incursion.

Transition

The peace force is expected to assist the parties in changing the status or condition of a country. A transition operation can be extremely difficult and highly intrusive, even to the extent of placing a country or parts of a country under temporary governance by the United Nations. Transition requires a high degree of consent—not just acquiescence but active cooperation in achieving the new status or condition.

The peace force may facilitate demobilization, arms limitations, referenda, national reconciliation, elections, and creation of new governmental forms. For example, the peace force may facilitate demobilization by establishing collection points, receiving and safeguarding arms, and protecting former soldiers during the process.

The Security Council has invoked both Chapter VI and Chapter VII for transition operations. Transition operations under Chapter VII are the usual origin of peace enforcement.

Security for Humanitarian Aid

The peace force is expected to secure humanitarian aid that alleviates suffering caused by conflict. The Force Commander's primary task is to secure aid—not to provide it—although he may also assist in providing it. Parties consent by agreeing not to obstruct humanitarian aid and to respect the force that secures it.

This type of operation extends only to humanitarian aid. Securing populations in safe areas or protected areas would exceed its bounds and imply a transition operation. Security of populations is the fundamental responsibility of a sovereign. The Security Council could not assume such responsibility indefinitely, unless it were to create an interminable trusteeship; therefore, it must look to an inevitable transition, e.g., resumption of power by a legitimate government, assumption of power by some newly created authority.

Security for aid goes beyond self-defense of the force; therefore, the Security Council, logically, should invoke Chapter VII. But on several occasions the Security Council has invoked Chapter VI for this type of operation.

Peace Enforcement

The peace force is expected to coerce recalcitrant parties into complying with their agreements or with resolutions of the Security Council. Normally, peace enforcement occurs in the context of an operation under Chapter VII when a party or parties withdraw consent and the Security Council decides to enforce its will. The critical decision is whether to invoke Chapter VII, not whether to attempt peace enforcement subsequently. Chapter VII implies willingness to coerce parties if they withdraw consent, putting the decision to attempt coercion in their hands.

There is a large practical difference between *peace enforcement*, which presumes impartiality, and *enforcement* against a uniquely identified aggressor: During peace enforcement, the Security Council precludes itself from allying with any party.

Overview of an Operational Typology

Peace operations, including variants of the basic types, are summarized in Figure S.1.

RAND*MR582-S.1*

	Observation		Interposition		Transition		Security for Humanitarian Aid	Peace Enforcement
Peace Operations								
	Peace-Keeping				**More-Ambitious Operations**			
	Facilitate agreement	Deter violations	Facilitate agreement	Deter violations	Transition		Security for Humanitarian Aid	Peace Enforcement
Chapter of the U.N. Charter	Chapter VI (self-defense)				Chapter VI (self-defense)	Chapter VII (potential enforcement)	Chapter VII (secure aid)	Chapter VII (enforce will of UNSC)
Consent Required from the Parties	Allow access to observers		Acquiesce in impartial control of a buffer zone		Cooperate in achieving new condition and status of a country		Allow provision of aid	None: occurs when party *withdraws* consent
Typical Mandate	Observe compliance with agreements; report violations; mediate among parties	Plus respond forcefully to violations	Create buffer zones; control entry into buffer zones; monitor arms limitations	Plus respond forcefully to violations	Provide secure conditions; oversee demobilization, demilitarization, arms limitations; provide security for electoral activities; facilitate reconstruction; cooperate closely with civilian component and NGOs		Provide security for humanitarian aid	Coerce recalcitrant parties into complying with UNSC resolutions and parties' agreements

|◄——————— Chapter VI ———————►|◄——————— Chapter VII ———————►|

Figure S.1—Peace Operations and Their Variants

EVALUATING PEACE OPERATIONS

The Security Council has often succeeded in traditional peace-keeping and has had some success in more-ambitious peace operations under Chapter VI. But the Council has failed repeatedly and sometimes catastrophically when it has attempted operations under Chapter VII, even when great powers participated.

Defining *Success*

From an operational perspective, *success* means fulfilling the mandate. The operation should be considered successful when it accomplishes the tasks implied by the mandate, even when conflict resumes for reasons beyond the control of the peace force. If, on the other hand, the peace force does not fulfill the mandate, either because it lacks required capabilities or because the parties refuse to cooperate, the operation should be considered a failure, whatever happens in the conflict.

To assume that an operation succeeded because the conflict subsided is to fall into a *post hoc, ergo propter hoc* fallacy. Almost every conflict will subside sooner or later, largely as a result of its own dynamics, whether or not there is any peace operation. Moreover, most peace operations are not coercive. They are intended to facilitate a process that parties agree to accomplish, not to coerce them; therefore, volition of the parties weighs more heavily than actions of the peace force. Even peace enforcement, decisive as it may be at the time, is only a temporary expedient.

Peace-Keeping

Traditional peace-keeping has helped parties to implement their agreements. It has tended to succeed when the agreements were viable, i.e., were concluded bona fide, because the parties believed the agreements were compatible with their interests and preferable to continuing a violent conflict.

But why should the Security Council be expected to help parties implement agreements that are in their own interests? There are several, often interrelated reasons:

- The parties may be so swayed by mutual animosity and suspicion that they need an impartial intermediary.
- Each party may hesitate to fulfill agreements unless it is reliably informed that other parties are also in compliance.
- The parties may be willing to disengage their forces, yet may be fearful that their adversaries will renege and gain advantages.

A peace-keeping force can allay these fears by controlling buffer zones that include strategically important terrain. In addition, peace-keeping can affect states that are not parties yet are interested in the outcome. For example, the great powers have used peace-keeping to help limit and contain their own rivalry, especially in the Middle East.

More-Ambitious Operations

Under Chapter VI. Transition operations under Chapter VI have tended to succeed once the parties had exhausted their hope of obtaining better results through violence and when other states had given active support to the peace process, keeping the parties under pressure to maintain their agreements. Operations in Namibia, Nicaragua, and Mozambique fit this pattern.

As might be anticipated, some parties reneged on their agreements when their power appeared threatened. Examples include the Pol Pot faction of the Khmer Rouge in Cambodia, *União Nacional para a Independência Total de Angola* (UNITA) in Angola, and Serbs in Croatia. In these examples, the Security Council deplored breaches of agreements but did not attempt to enforce compliance. It allowed parts of the original mandate to fall into abeyance (Cambodia), terminated the peace operation (Angola), or accepted a lesser mandate before the U.N. operation was swept away (Croatia). While such behavior may appear ignoble for an organization with the authority of the Security Council, it is surely preferable to half-hearted attempts at enforcement.

Under Chapter VII. By invoking Chapter VII, the Security Council has indicated a willingness to apply force, if necessary, to coerce parties that defy its resolutions. The Council has therefore assumed the role of a potential combatant, compelling the parties to assess the probable consequences if they oppose the Council. Parties were unlikely to defy the Council if they believed it had the political will and the military force to coerce them successfully. Such deterrence occurred when the United States deployed powerful forces under its own control (Multinational Force in Haiti, Unified Task Force in Somalia). Although international in a formal sense, these operations were fundamentally U.S. initiatives conducted under authority of the Security Council.

Absent strong U.S. participation, the Security Council has neither demonstrated the political will nor assembled the military force needed to coerce parties. Perceiving this weakness, parties have ignored resolutions under Chapter VII and have openly defied the Council. Examples include Mohammed Farah Aideed's faction in Mogadishu and the Bosnian Serb authorities in Pale. In these instances, the Council made half-hearted attempts at peace enforcement and suffered ignominious failures.

Peace enforcement has failed for the same reason that collective security has failed: lack of a sufficiently strong consensus for action among permanent members of the Security Council. Moreover, peace enforcement has special complications and difficulties. Complications ensue because more than one party can be recalcitrant, either successively or simultaneously. For example, Bosnian Muslims and Bosnian Serbs both violated provisions concerning safe areas, although the Serb violations were more egregious. Difficulties arise because impartiality demands that the Security Council forgo the benefits of having allies among parties to the conflict. In the same example, it was precluded from arming and training Bosnian Muslim forces to resist attacks on safe areas.

USEFULNESS OF THE TYPOLOGY

An operational perspective generates a useful typology of peace operations. Such a typology promotes a differentiated view, allows fruitful comparisons among operations of similar type, and provides a point of departure for reform.

A Differentiated View

It is tempting to idealize peace operations at one extreme or to denigrate them at the other. Those who believe that a responsible international community exists or can be created are inclined to romanticize peace operations. To a sympathetic observer, the mere appearance of a peace operation is immensely appealing. Contingents from many states join forces not to fight a war for national interests, but to promote peace for the common good. But those who believe that a responsible international community is fantasy or an undesirable trammel are inclined to denigrate peace operations. To an unsympathetic eye, they seem an excuse to remunerate impecunious states—at best a make-work project and at worst a pious hoax.

There is little point in undifferentiated praise or condemnation. Peace operations will not bring in the millennium, but they can make valuable contributions to peace. These contributions should be understood in the context of an operational typology. Some types of operations, especially those associated with traditional peace-keeping, have been competently performed through the U.N. system and have been well worth the expense. Other types of operations, especially those under Chapter VII that went to peace enforcement, have demanded more commitment from great powers than those powers were willing to make and have brought costly failures. The primary cause of these failures was lack of determination among the great powers, not some failing of the admittedly imperfect U.N. or some inherent flaw in peace operations.

Fruitful Comparisons

The typology presented in this report allows fruitful comparisons among peace operations of the same type. It is fruitful, for example, to review the records of observer forces to discern what activities are accessible to observation, what reconnaissance means are required, and how much cooperation is needed from the parties. Comparisons are also helpful when they reveal prerequisites for success and root causes of failure. Particularly instructive are comparisons among transition operations, a type that has burgeoned in past years, involves complex mandates, and demands close coordination with numerous civilian organizations.

Comparing operations of the same type can support efforts to develop rapid response within the U.N. system. It appears unlikely that the Security Council will ever command large-scale forces commensurate with its responsibilities under Chapter VII. But the Council may well have small-scale forces at its disposal that are ready to conduct the repertoire of traditional peace-keeping under Chapter VI. Comparison of past operations should allow planners to discern accurately what organization, equipment, and training would be appropriate for such forces undertaking a particular type of operation.

Basis for Reform

Peace operations must be reformed; otherwise, their future will be very bleak. By early 1996, the Security Council was suffering a severe loss of reputation through humiliating failures in places such as Mogadishu and Srebrenica. At the same time, the U.N. system was plunged into financial crisis by refusal of member states, especially the United States, to pay their assessments. These two developments were related: Congressional reluctance to pay for peace operations was deepened by failures, especially what was seen as betrayal of the Bosnian Muslims.

The most urgent reform is for the Security Council to see peace operations from an operational perspective rather than a largely political perspective. In recent years, the Council has passed far more resolutions than previously, including many that the parties have ignored. Being ignored is problematic because it diminishes the prestige of the Security Council. But the Council has done far greater harm by giving unrealistic mandates to Force Commanders. An operational perspective on peace operations should help decision-makers to frame mandates that are appropriate to the situation and to the capabilities of the peace force.

ACKNOWLEDGMENTS

The authors gratefully acknowledge the help of colleagues at RAND. Arnold Kanter provided overall guidance and reviewed the formal briefing prepared during Phase One. As leader of "Operational Strategies for Peace Enforcement," Bruce Bennett helped to provide the intellectual framework. Arthur Bullock prepared useful case studies of peace operations in Cambodia and the Congo. Ted Karasik provided valuable research assistance. Richard Darilek contributed insights into peace operations on the Golan Heights. Steve Hosmer commented on peace operations from his wide understanding of military affairs. Robert Howe informally reviewed work conducted during Phase One of this project. Dean Millot advised on points of international law. Marten van Heuven reviewed an initial draft of this document.

The head of RAND's Washington office, David Chu, helped to finance Bruce Pirnie's participation in a tour of peace operations in the former Yugoslavia during June 3–10, 1994, which was conducted by the United Nations Association of the United States of America. The Association's Vice President, Ralph Cwerman, ably organized that tour.

The authors extend thanks to Sarah B. Sewall, Deputy Assistant Secretary of Defense for Peacekeeping and Peace Enforcement Policy, for her constructive criticism throughout the project and for sponsoring a series of briefings that provoked helpful comments. They thank the project monitor, Lee Feinstein, who helped to redefine the project and saw it to a successful conclusion despite his reassignment. They thank Leonard Hawley and Kenneth Handelman in the same office for offering constructive criticism and assisting in a series of briefings given to interested persons in the U.N. Department of Peace-Keeping Operations, State Department, U.S. Mission to the United Nations, National Security Council, Central Intelligence Agency, Department of Defense, Joint Staff, Defense Intelligence Agency, Army Staff, and the U.S. Army Training and Doctrine Command at Fort Monroe, Virginia.

William J. Durch, Senior Associate at the Henry L. Stimson Center and author of *The Evolution of UN Peacekeeping: Case Studies and Comparative Analysis*, an authoritative source of information and insights on peace operations, kindly reviewed the manuscript in draft. The authors profited greatly from Bill's perceptive comments. Marian Branch edited the final draft very skillfully, improving the report. Full responsibility for any errors in fact or judgment remains with the authors.

ACRONYMS AND ABBREVIATIONS

CINCCENT	Commander in Chief, Central Command [United States]
CINCUNC	Commander in Chief, United Nations Command [Korea]
FMLN	*Frente Farabundo Martí para la Liberación Nacional*
FUNCINPEC	United Front for an Independent, Neutral, Peaceful, and Cooperative Cambodia [Royalist party]
IFOR	Implementation Force
JCS	Joint Chiefs of Staff
KPNLF	Khmer People's National Liberation Front [alliance of pro–Lon Nol elements]
MINURSO	United Nations Mission for the Referendum in Western Sahara
NATO	North Atlantic Treaty Organization
NGO	Non-governmental organization
OAU	Organization of African Unity
ONUC	*Operation des Nations Unies au Congo* (United Nations Operation in the Congo [the former Belgian Congo]
ONUCA	United Nations Observer Group in Central America [Costa Rica, El Salvador, Guatemala, Honduras, Nicaragua]
ONUMOZ	United Nations Operation in Mozambique
PDK	Party of Democratic Kampuchea [Pol Pot faction of Khmer Rouge]
PLO	Palestine Liberation Organization

[*Frente*] POLISARIO	*Frente Popular para la Liberación de Saguia el-Hamra y de Rio de Oro* [an independence movement that declared the Sahrawi Arab Democratic Republic]
RPF	Rwandan Patriotic Front
SWAPO	South West African People's Organization
U.N.	United Nations
UNAMIC	United Nations Advance Mission in Cambodia
UNAMIR	United Nations Assistance Mission for Rwanda
UNAVEM I	First United Nations Angola Verification Mission [Angola and Namibia]
UNAVEM II	Second United Nations Angola Verification Mission
UNCRO	United Nations Confidence Restoration Operation in Croatia
UNDOF	United Nations Disengagement Observer Force [Golan Heights]
UNEF I	First United Nations Emergency Force [Gaza and Sinai]
UNEF II	Second United Nations Emergency Force [Sinai]
UNFICYP	United Nations Peace-Keeping Force in Cyprus
UNGOMAP	United Nations Good Offices Mission in Afghanistan and Pakistan [Afghanistan and Pakistan]
UNIFIL	United Nations Interim Force in Lebanon [southern Lebanon]
UNIIMOG	United Nations Iran-Iraq Military Observer Group
UNIKOM	United Nations Iraq-Kuwait Observer Mission
UNITA	*União Nacional para a Independência Total de Angola* (National Union for the Complete Independence of Angola)
UNITAF	Unified Task Force [Somalia]
UNMIH	United Nations Mission in Haiti
UNMOGIP	United Nations Military Observer Group in India and Pakistan [Jammu and Kashmir]
UNOGIL	United Nations Observation Group in Lebanon [Lebanon]
UNOSOM I	First United Nations Operation in Somalia
UNOSOM II	Second United Nations Operation in Somalia
UNPA	United Nations Protected Area [generally Serb-held areas of Croatia]

UNPF	United Nations Peace Force [U.N. forces in the former Yugoslavia from March 1995]
UNPREDEP	United Nations Preventive Deployment Force [Macedonia]
UNPROFOR	United Nations Protection Force [the former Yugoslavia]
UNSC	United Nations Security Council
UNTAC	United Nations Transitional Authority in Cambodia
UNTAES	United Nations Transitional Administration for Eastern Slavonia, Baranja and Western Sirmium [Serb-held area of Croatia west of Dunav (Danube) River, formerly Sector East]
UNTAG	United Nations Transition Assistance Group [Namibia]
UNTEA/UNSF	United Nations Temporary Executive Authority/ United Nations Security Force in West New Guinea (West Irian)
UNTSO	United Nations Truce Supervision Organization [Near East]
UNYOM	United Nations Yemen Observation Mission [Saudi-Yemen border]
U.S.	United States
USCENTCOM	United States Central Command
WWII	World War II

Chapter One

INTRODUCTION

PURPOSE OF THE STUDY

Peace operations do not appear in the Charter of the United Nations; rather, they evolved through ad hoc responses to conflict.[1] Nor has the United Nations promulgated authoritative doctrine for peace operations as, for example, the U.S. armed services do for combat operations. As a result, the subject of peace operations is plagued by imprecise definitions. Even the most fundamental terms are inconsistently or vaguely defined, including *consent* and *impartiality*, which set the boundary between peace operations and other uses of military force.[2]

Such imprecision makes peace operations more difficult to conduct successfully and tends to discredit them. Indeed, there is much truth in widespread criticism that the larger peace operations in particular have become murky and ill-defined. This report attempts to promote clarity by defining terms precisely and developing a typology of peace operations across the spectrum. This typology is intended as a practical guide based on the accumulated experience of five decades

---

[1] "A way had to be found to stop hostilities and to control conflicts so that they would not develop into broader conflagrations. Out of that need, United Nations peace-keeping operations evolved as, essentially, holding actions. There was not, and still is not, any particular theory or doctrine behind them. They were born of necessity, largely improvised, a practical response to a problem requiring action." United Nations, *The Blue Helmets: A Review of United Nations Peace-Keeping*, Department of Public Information, New York, 1990, p. 4.

[2] Definitions of terms associated with peace operations are presented in Appendix A.

of peace operations conducted under authority of the United Nations.

STUDY APPROACH

This study uses a quasi-historical method to develop an operationally oriented typology.

Quasi-Historical Method

We call the method *quasi-historical* because many of the peace operations used to build the typology belong to current events, not to history.   Decades will pass before permanent members of the Security Council, other participating member states, and parties to conflicts open their archives to researchers. Years, if not decades, will pass before individual actors present memoirs that may shed more light on their motivations and influence on events. Historians will also need time to exploit new materials and to arrive at well-considered judgments.   Moreover, the eventual course of some important peace operations, especially those in Bosnia-Herzegovina, is still uncertain.   But we already know enough to draw some conclusions and cannot afford to wait on events.

Eschewing a more theoretical approach imposes some limitations on the study. The record of peace operations imposes the most obvious limitation: While extremely rich and varied, it may not exhaust the possibilities. In recent years, permanent members of the Security Council (excepting the People's Republic of China) have participated more frequently and on a larger scale than they had previously. Their participation raises the prospect of conducting coercive peace operations more successfully. The first rush of post–Cold War enthusiasm was misguided, producing dramatic and humiliating disasters. But if the hard lessons are absorbed, the permanent members may yet expand the possibilities of peace operations. For example, the Implementation Force (IFOR) currently enforces a buffer zone between parties, offering to coerce any party that attempts to enter the zone contrary to the Dayton Agreements. Coercive interposition is an innovation in peace operations, even within the context of an ambitious mandate.

In addition, the study uses terms that are rooted in accounts of peace operations—so firmly rooted that they would be difficult to dislodge. Some of these terms are felicitous; others are liable to misinterpretation no matter how assiduously we define them. Two prominent examples are "peace-keeping" and "peace enforcement."

Traditional "peace-keeping" operations do not *keep* peace: They merely *facilitate* some agreements that may promote peace. Whether peace ensues or war breaks out depends primarily on the parties, not on the peace operation. "Peace enforcement" is liable to misinterpretation because it is so easily confused with "enforcement," a much different undertaking. But for the time being, it is better to use existing terms than to risk confusion by trying to introduce new ones.

Operational Perspective

Peace operations are highly political. But they should also make operational sense; otherwise, military forces should not be employed. The conflict may be imperfectly understood and still evolving. The permanent members may have divergent views that must be carefully balanced. The language of diplomacy and political discourse is rich in shadings and nuances to accommodate divergent views and still allow common action. The Security Council may have to express the goal of a peace operation in broad language and artfully ambiguous words. But the decision to initiate a peace operation has practical consequences that also demand an operational perspective. Some peace force will be in the field, usually one ready for combat at least in self-defense, and it should be given reasonably clear orders.

This typology looks at peace operations very much as a Force Commander must. With as much precision as the subject allows, this typology defines peace operations in ways that he would find helpful. A Force Commander needs to know what difference his operation is expected to make, what tasks he must perform, what authorization he has to employ lethal force, and how much cooperation he should expect from the parties. From this operational perspective, distinctions among *keeping, making, building,* and *enforcing* a hazily defined condition called "peace" are confusing or irrelevant.[3]   The Force Commander needs a mandate ("mission" in military usage) that he can translate into action.

Precise Typology Versus Messy Execution

Peace operations usually become messy because the peace force is not strong enough to impose its will and therefore is buffeted by the parties. A Force Commander may find that the parties are effusive in their expressions of support and obstructive in their actions. He may find that they are maneuvering for their own advantages rather than promoting a peace process. Some provisions of his mandate may be unworkable, and new tasks may emerge that did not appear in the original mandate.

But messy execution does not justify an imprecise typology. On the contrary, an expectation of messiness increases the need for a precise typology. A Force Commander is better able to handle the shocks and frustrations of field operations when he understands what he is expected to accomplish. Moreover, a precise typology can inform decisions at higher levels.

For example, a decision to employ lethal force is seldom easy. A Force Commander must balance the responsibility to protect his force with the need to avoid escalation that could worsen the situation. He may have to demonstrate forbearance, yet avoid an impression of weakness that would encourage obstructive behavior from the parties. But this inherent difficulty does not suggest that the Security Council or a Special Representative of the Secretary-General should obscure the difference between "blue helmet" and "green helmet" operations. Either the peace force is a noncombatant that makes itself conspicuous to avoid inadvertent encounters ("blue helmet") or it is a potential combatant that camouflages itself to sur-

---

[3]Secretary-General of the United Nations, Boutros Boutros-Ghali, formulated a typology using these terms, in United Nations, *Preventive Diplomacy, Peacemaking and Peace-Keeping: Report of the Secretary-General Pursuant to the Statement Adopted by the Summit Meeting of the Security Council on 31 January 1992*, A/47/277, S/24111, New York, June 17, 1992; hereafter *Agenda for Peace—1992*. See Appendix B for excerpts from that report.

vive ("green helmet"). Trying to obscure this difference exasperates the Force Commander and appears hypocritical to the parties.

USE OF THIS TYPOLOGY

This typology should help decisionmakers to understand the limitations of peace operations, to select the optimal type of operation for a given situation, and to evaluate the success of an operation.

Understanding the Limitations

An operationally oriented typology directs attention to the limitations of peace operations. Peace operations are a limited application of military force that is not intended to achieve decisive results. Usually, they are intended to facilitate agreements that parties have concluded in their own interests but need help to implement. Even peace operations that employ overwhelming force are limited by the period of time that the peace forces remain deployed. After they depart, resolution of conflict depends once more on the parties and the peoples concerned.

To appreciate the limitations of peace operations, it is instructive to contrast them with major wars. When the United States conducts major wars, it usually intends to achieve decisive results that will ensure accomplishment of its political goals. When the United States and its allies in World War II (WWII) defeated the Axis powers, Western Europe was liberated and the fascist threat was removed; there was little prospect that fascism could survive defeat. In strong contrast, a peace operation might succeed completely, accomplishing every provision of the mandate, yet still not achieve the political goal of resolving conflict. After termination of the United Nations Mission in Haiti (UNMIH), Haiti might fall back into a cycle of rapacious government and violent revolt. After departure of IFOR, the parties in the former Yugoslavia might descend once more into protracted, inconclusive, and highly destructive conflict. Only if the Security Council deployed overwhelming force indefinitely could peace operations achieve decisive results in the sense that major wars do.

Selecting the Optimal Type of Operation

This typology should also help decisionmakers to select an optimal type of operation either at the outset or when an existing operation needs revision. It offers a spectrum of operations, each with its typical requirements for consent from the parties and support from those member states that choose to participate. From this spectrum, decisionmakers should select the type of operation optimal for the situation and within the range of expected support from member states.

For example, in early May 1994, the Secretary-General wanted to stop genocide in Rwanda by enforcing peace, but the United States refused to assent to such an operation unless member states were willing to contribute the required forces. On May 17, the United States agreed to expand the mandate of the United Nations Assistance Mission for Rwanda (UNAMIR) more cautiously to include "security and protection of displaced persons, refugees and civilians at risk in Rwanda."[4] UNAMIR was subsequently authorized a strength of 5,500 troops. But this force, consisting primarily of African contingents, would take time to assemble. To respond more rapidly, the Security Council authorized France to lead a unilateral operation under national control (Operation Turquoise), which offered some protection to civilians in government-held areas until the Rwandan Patriotic Front seized control in August.

Evaluating a Peace Operation

This typology also suggests how peace operations should be evaluated. It would be incorrect to evaluate them simply by whether the conflict was resolved. Resolution of conflict, i.e., an enduring political settlement, depends more on the parties and peoples concerned than upon peace operations. Therefore, evaluation should consider (1) whether the operation itself is successful and (2) how much its success contributes to resolving the conflict.

The first question is whether the operation itself is successful. Like any military operation, it should be accounted a success when the

---

[4]Security Council Resolution 918, May 17, 1994.

commander accomplishes his mission, or in the parlance of peace operations, when the Force Commander fulfills his mandate. For example, the second United Nations Operation in Somalia (UNOSOM II) clearly failed to fulfill its ambitious mandate (to collect weapons in accordance with the Addis Ababa agreements, arrest those responsible for armed attacks on the peace force, and secure humanitarian aid) and should be considered a failure even had the warring factions somehow come to terms through their own volition. Similarly, the United Nations Protection Force (UNPROFOR) did not accomplish the most important tasks contained in its mandate (enforcing a no-fly zone, seeing that safe areas are free from armed attack, and enforcing exclusion zones) and therefore was largely a failure. It should not be judged successful because the parties concluded the Dayton Agreements, an event largely unrelated to UNPROFOR's performance.

The second question is how much the success of a peace operation contributes to conflict resolution. The answer usually demands expert judgments concerning highly complex situations. For example, the United Nations Operation in Mozambique (ONUMOZ) made an important contribution to resolving a protracted civil war; however, success was due also to political pressure exerted by outside powers and to exhaustion of the combatants.

In several cases, successful peace operations have done little or nothing to resolve the conflict. The First United Nations Emergency Force (UNEF I) successfully interposed itself between Egypt and Israel in 1956, but these countries went to war again in 1967. The United Nations Peace-Keeping Force in Cyprus (UNFICYP) successfully controls a buffer zone across the island. UNFICYP undoubtedly contributes to stability in Cyprus by separating Greek and Turkish Cypriots, but their conflict is no closer to resolution today than it was over 20 years ago, when the buffer zone was first established.

CONDUCT OF THE PROJECT

The project was accomplished in two phases: Phase One from September through October 1994, and Phase Two from November through December 1994. This report encapsulates results from Phase One.

Phase One

In Phase One, we developed a typology of peace operations. Our method was to review past and current operations, posing the question: What was the force expected to accomplish? This question is posed from the perspective of a Special Representative of the Secretary-General or a Force Commander who must understand his mandate in practical terms. The results of Phase One are contained in this report.

Phase Two

In Phase Two, we developed a set of critical issues across the spectrum of peace operations, using the same quasi-historical method. We posed the question: What issues had the largest impact on success or failure of the operation? We organized these issues under six broad headings: nature of the conflict, consent of the parties to the conflict, mandate, character of the peace force, physical environment, and support from states that were not parties. *Consent*, defined as the evident willingness of parties to help accomplish a mandate, is a complex phenomenon of quicksilver character, itself worth a volume. The results of Phase Two are reported in MR-583-OSD, *Soldiers for Peace: Critical Operational Issues*, 1996.

Information Cutoff

Research for this project was completed in spring 1995. The authors have generally retained this information cutoff date, with the notable exception of operations in the former Yugoslavia. The collapse of the exclusion zone around Sarajevo in June, the fall of Srebrenica in July, the invasion of Krajina in August, and the successful NATO bombing campaign in September are so well-known and instructive that the authors had to include them.

Chapter Two

DEFINING PEACE OPERATIONS

This chapter defines peace operations, including their relationship to the Charter of the United Nations, the criteria that distinguish peace operations from other uses of force, and the issue of domestic jurisdiction.

CHARTER OF THE UNITED NATIONS

The Charter of the United Nations describes a system of collective security with two modalities: pacific settlement, outlined in Chapter VI, and action with respect to threats to the peace, described in Chapter VII.

Chapter VI

Chapter VI is directed toward the peaceful resolution of disputes that are likely to endanger peace. It lists traditional techniques of diplomacy, including negotiation, inquiry, mediation, conciliation, arbitration, judicial settlement, resort to regional agencies or arrangements, and other peaceful means. To these techniques it adds the organs of the United Nations itself, including the Security Council, the General Assembly, and the International Court of Justice.

Chapter VII

Chapter VII outlines forceful ways of dealing with threats to peace, breaches of peace, and acts of aggression. Article 40 empowers the Security Council to call upon parties to comply with provisional measures it deems necessary or desirable. Article 42 empowers the Council to take action using air, land, and sea forces to maintain or restore international peace and security. Article 43 outlines how member states will make forces available to the Security Council.

Article 45 requires member states to hold air forces immediately available for enforcement. Article 47 requires establishment of a Military Staff Committee composed of the Chiefs of Staff of the five permanent members of the Security Council or their representatives to advise and assist the Council.

In 1947, representatives of the Permanent Five discussed implementation of Article 43. The United States recommended that the members provide forces appropriate for a major regional contingency.[1] However, with the Cold War already in progress, the Permanent Five could not reach agreement.

Collective security under Chapter VII depends on the five permanent members of the Security Council, essentially the winning coalition in WWII. Implicitly recognizing that enforcement must be compatible with their interests, they have a veto power.[2] Collective security requires that the Permanent Five remain at peace among themselves and that they enforce peace upon the lesser powers, thus perpetuating the wartime coalition in a new form.

Although the Permanent Five have remained at peace among themselves,[3] their interests have not converged sufficiently to make col-

---

[1]Specifically, the U.S. representative recommended 20 ground divisions, 1,250 bombers, 2,250 fighters, and 6 aircraft carriers, plus large numbers of other surface combatants. In contrast, the Soviet Union recommended 12 ground divisions, 600 bombers, 300 fighters, and no aircraft carriers, plus smaller numbers of other surface combatants than the United States. The United States argued that the Permanent Five should contribute according to their capabilities; the Soviet Union argued for equal contributions. Underlying these disagreements was fundamental political divergence between the Western democracies and the Communist dictatorships.

[2]Article 27 contains the veto power. It provides that on all matters that are not procedural, decisions of the Security Council require concurring votes of the permanent members, except that in decisions under Chapter VI and under Article 52 (pacific settlement through regional agencies), parties to a dispute abstain from voting.

[3]The People's Republic of China and the United States fought during 1950–1953, but during that time Taiwan held the permanent seat on the Security Council reserved for China. In protest against this seating of Nationalist China, the representative of the

lective security practicable. Perhaps the closest approach was their agreement in November 1990 to authorize member states to use "all necessary means" to effect the withdrawal of Iraqi forces from Kuwait.[4] But in this instance, as earlier in Korea, the United States dominated operations and would likely have acted from its national interests had the Security Council made no decision. Korea and Kuwait certainly demonstrate that the U.N. can help advance U.S. interests and the interests of its allies, but these operations have much less relevance to collective security.

CRITERIA THAT BOUND PEACE OPERATIONS

Over the past five decades, the Security Council developed peace operations, an ad hoc response to conflict. Peace operations were not presented in the Charter or derived from any theory; rather, they developed in response to the exigencies of conflict.

Neither Chapter VI nor Chapter VII of the Charter addresses peace operations. Recognizing that these operations fall somewhere between diplomacy and use of force, Secretary-General Dag Hammarskjöld observed wryly that they might be described in a new "Chapter Six and a Half."[5] In practice, the Security Council has invoked both Chapter VI and Chapter VII in the context of peace operations. Invoking Chapter VI has implied that lethal force is authorized in self-defense while accomplishing the mandate. Invoking Chapter VII has implied that lethal force is authorized to accomplish the mandate, coercing parties if necessary. However, actual performance in the field has varied widely from case to case.[6]

Soviet Union had left his seat. Had the Soviet representative been present, he would doubtless have vetoed the resolution creating the United Nations Command in Korea.

[4]Security Council Resolution 678, adopted on November 29, 1990.

[5]United Nations, *The Blue Helmets*, 1990, p. 5.

[6]In Somalia, the Unified Task Force (UNITAF) had Chapter VII authorization and frequently used lethal force beyond strict self-defense to ensure passage of humanitarian aid and to compel limited disarmament. In Bosnia, the United Nations Protection Force (UNPROFOR) had Chapter VII authorization but used lethal force only in self-defense. (However, NATO, acting in tandem with UNPROFOR, conducted air attacks on the Bosnian Serbs.) These discrepancies between authorization and actual use of force were due to relative combat power: UNITAF had overwhelming force; UNPROFOR was weak and vulnerable to retaliation.

Although remarkably diverse, all peace operations presupposed at least initial consent of the parties and impartiality by the Security Council. Therefore, consent and impartiality[7] became criteria to define the domain of peace operations.

Consent of the Parties

Parties are entities that the Security Council believes are responsible for conflict, implying that they control significantly large forces, but not that they have any particular legal status. At some point in the conflict, the entities usually acquire the status of parties to agreements, the origin of the term "parties." Parties have included clan leaders (Somalia), self-declared governments (Bosnian Serb authority in Pale), and, of course, member states in the United Nations.

Consent means that parties to a conflict are willing to help accomplish the mandate. Consent ranges from grudging acquiescence to enthusiastic acceptance. For example, the Cédras regime in Haiti gave its consent under duress to avoid a U.S. invasion. Bosnian Serbs repeatedly gave formal consent, although it may well be doubted whether they ever really consented to an operation they suspected was directed against themselves. In contrast, Bosnian Muslims gave nearly full consent and were primarily aggrieved that the peace force did so little to accomplish its mandate.

It is very common for parties to cooperate fully with provisions of the mandate they believe will advance their aims while impeding accomplishment of less-welcome provisions. Consent also usually varies over the course of an operation. For example, Croatia initially gave reluctant consent to an operation on its territory but became increasingly disaffected, finally attacking and killing several U.N.

---

[7]"The United Nations can be proud of the speed with which peace-keeping has evolved in response to the new political environment resulting from the end of the cold war, but the last few years have confirmed that respect for certain basic principles of peace-keeping [is] essential to its success. Three particularly important principles are the consent of the parties, impartiality and the non-use of force except in self-defence." United Nations, *Supplement to An Agenda for Peace: Position Paper of the Secretary-General on the Occasion of the Fiftieth Anniversary of the United Nations*, A/50/60, S/1995/1, New York, January 3, 1995, Paragraph 33; hereafter, *Agenda for Peace—1995*.

soldiers and causing the Security Council to terminate operations on Croatian territory, except in Eastern Slavonia.

To date, no peace operation has been initiated without at least initial consent from the parties.[8] In some future case, the Security Council might proceed without consent to carry out peace enforcement. Serious practical difficulties are associated with such an operation. But since great powers have begun to participate more extensively in peace operations, the possibility of an operation without initial consent cannot be excluded.

Impartiality

Impartiality means that the Security Council has decided not to take sides, judging that all parties share responsibility for a conflict; it identifies neither aggressor nor victim. Not taking sides implies that the Council will not try to attain the political-military aims of any one party to the exclusion of other parties' aims. During peace enforcement, the Council maintains impartiality by employing force against *any* party that shows itself to be recalcitrant.

To use a current example, IFOR is authorized to employ force against any party—whether Croat, Muslim, or Serb—that fails to comply with certain provisions of the Dayton Agreements. If any party violated the Dayton Agreements, and NATO, acting under authority of the Security Council, employed force against that party, neither NATO nor the Council would become partial for that reason. As with police in all democratic states, they are expected to enforce the law

---

[8]Recent operations in Haiti illustrate this point. If the United States had invaded Haiti under authority of the Security Council, this operation would have satisfied neither criterion of a peace operation; it would have been enforcement. But just as the United States had begun to launch an invasion, the Cédras regime conveyed its consent to a delegation led by former President Jimmy Carter. This consent was reluctant, belated, and obtained under duress of imminent attack—but was consent nevertheless. In this case, the party granting consent was a regime considered illegitimate and reprehensible by the Security Council. When the Cédras regime dissolved itself as promised, the Aristide government naturally consented to an operation that had restored and now supported its authority. The criterion of impartiality was rendered moot by the demise of the Cédras regime. Once it vanished, there were no parties in Haiti, only the sole legitimate government without any rival or opponent for the Security Council to consider.

impartially, which implies that they will use force against any violator of the law.

Parties tend to believe that they are treated unfairly and to accuse the peace force of favoring other parties. They may insist that all actions of the peace force be neutral in their effect, i.e., affect all parties equally. But even the least intrusive peace operation is highly unlikely to affect all parties equally. Consider, for example, an operation involving unarmed military observers. That operation would affect all parties equally if all parties were equally liable to commit violations, if the likelihood of detection were equal for all violations, and if the consequences of detection were identical for all parties. While theoretically possible, such a case is so wildly improbable that it can be dismissed.

If the Security Council judges that the parties do not share responsibility but, rather, that there is an aggressor who bears all the responsibility, it may authorize a range of actions directed against the aggressor, as in Korea and Kuwait. Peace operations, by definition, are precluded in such a situation.

ISSUE OF DOMESTIC JURISDICTION

Within the bounds of consent and impartiality, other delimiting factors are blurred. Chief among these is the distinction between *domestic jurisdiction* and the *international sphere.* The first purpose of the U.N. is "to maintain international peace and security" (Article 1), so the Charter of the United Nations limits collective security to the international sphere. It is an organization "based on the principle of the sovereign equality of all its Members" (Article 2); therefore, the members are enjoined not to use force "against the territorial integrity or political independence of any state" (Article 2). The U.N. is not authorized to intervene "in matters which are essentially within the domestic jurisdiction of any state" (Article 2); however, the distinction between international relations and domestic jurisdiction has become increasingly obscure from the vantage point of the Security Council.

The Charter recognizes the "equal rights and self-determination of peoples" (Article 1), but it may be difficult to define the entities that have these rights. For example, do Croats, Muslims, and Serbs in

Bosnia-Herzegovina constitute "peoples" in the sense of the Charter? During 1995, the Security Council and a Contact Group of great powers promoted a plan to divide Bosnia-Herzegovina among Croats, Muslims, and Serbs, in effect treating them as "peoples"—even though Bosnia-Herzegovina was a sovereign state and member of the United Nations. In this case, conflict within a member state was handled *as though* it were an international conflict.

The situation is even less clear when a state is wracked by conflict among faction leaders contending for national leadership. For example, 13 or 14 faction leaders were represented in the Addis Ababa conferences to promote national reconciliation in Somalia. Although the factions were based on clans, none of the faction leaders claimed to represent a separate people with the individual right of self-determination. But the Security Council treated even those faction leaders as parties to a conflict. In helping to implement their agreements, the Security Council assumed a broad authority to advance the development of a state, analogous to the authority it once exercised under the Trusteeship Council.[9]

In recent years, the Security Council has authorized peace operations in states suffering internal conflicts, even when there was little or no military threat to international peace and security. Haiti and Somalia, for example, did not threaten neighboring states, nor were neighboring states likely to be drawn into their internal conflicts. As a practical matter, the definition of *international peace and security* has widened to include such phenomena as refugee flows and catastrophic suffering caused by conflict. Such widening gives the Security Council very broad latitude for determining when to authorize a peace operation.

---

[9]Chapter XIII of the Charter establishes a Trusteeship Council composed of the permanent members of the Security Council and those members administering trust territories, plus an equal number of members not so charged. Its general purpose is to monitor conditions in trust territories. The last trust territory to become independent was Namibia in 1990. South Africa had administered Namibia under the League of Nations and refused to submit to the Trusteeship Council, despite a decision by the International Court of Justice requiring it to do so.

Chapter Three

SPECTRUM OF PEACE OPERATIONS

This chapter presents an operational typology of peace operations that is based on what the Force Commander is expected to accomplish and on his authorization to employ lethal force.

AN OPERATIONAL TYPOLOGY

The purpose of an operational typology is not to pigeonhole operations, i.e., demand that they conform to some preconceived, abstract notions. Rather, the purpose is to describe the scope and purpose of operations in a clear and consistent way to support decisionmaking. The resulting typology presents a spectrum to assist selection of the most appropriate and feasible type of peace operation for a given situation. It focuses attention on the implications of selecting a particular type of operation.

Peace operations have their origin in diplomacy, when parties may consent to a mandate and approve a peace plan. Beyond peace operations lies enforcement against a uniquely identified aggressor. Therefore, peace operations occupy a middle ground between diplomacy and enforcement, as follows:

- Diplomacy: avert, allay, or resolve conflict through negotiation, including acceptance of a peace operation.
- Peace operations:
  - Observation: observe, report, and mediate violations.
  - Interposition: control a buffer zone.

— Transition: help parties to change the status and condition
   of a country.

— Security for humanitarian aid: secure delivery, storage, and
   distribution of aid.

— Peace enforcement: compel recalcitrant parties to comply
   with their agreements or Security Council resolutions
   through combat operations.[1]

• Enforcement: maintain or restore peace and security through
  combat operations against a uniquely identified aggressor.

The following sections describe each type of peace operation and
give illustrative examples.

DIPLOMACY

Peace operations begin at the diplomatic level, with the initial consent of the parties. The Security Council and others acting with its
approval often try to promote pacific settlement through negotiations. During such negotiations, the parties may consent to a peace
operation that becomes integral to their agreement.

As an example, UNPROFOR was an integral part of the agreement
mediated by Cyrus Vance, Special Envoy of the Secretary-General, on
November 23, 1991, to end conflict in Croatia. Yugoslavia (Serbia
and Montenegro) was encouraged to conclude this agreement because UNPROFOR had a mandate to protect Serbs living in Croatia.
Croatia was encouraged, because UNPROFOR also had a mandate to
disarm the Croatian Serbs, a step Croatia hoped would lead to
restoration of its authority, peacefully or through force. The Croatian
Serbs had little confidence that UNPROFOR would protect them and
assented to the agreement only under strong pressure from Belgrade.

---

[1]Historically, peace enforcement has occurred as the result of a party's refusal to
accept some transition. Transition operations are an obvious source of peace
enforcement, because they are difficult and intrusive. But the Security Council might
initiate peace enforcement from any other type of operation.

UNPROFOR could not satisfy such divergent expectations, and it was vilified by all parties until Croatian offensives ended its existence.[2]

PEACE OPERATIONS

Observation and interposition together make up the repertoire of traditional peace-keeping. Transition, security for humanitarian aid, and peace enforcement go beyond traditional peace-keeping and are therefore considered more-ambitious operations. Peace enforcement occurs when the Security Council responds forcefully to recalcitrance during operations conducted under Chapter VII.

Observation

In this type of operation, the peace force is expected to monitor compliance with agreements, international law, or resolutions of the Security Council; report violations; and often mediate resolution of violations among the parties.

Observation is the most frequently undertaken, least intrusive, and least expensive peace operation. The observers are usually active or retired military officers. They may be unarmed, relying on the parties for their security, or they may be lightly armed for self-defense. Observation often implies mediation as well, because observers are uniquely positioned to serve as mediators.

There are two subtypes of observation, each having different implications for decisionmakers. The first subtype is intended to help implement agreement among the parties. There is no implied commitment that the Security Council will respond in any particular way if violations occur. The second subtype, which is intended to deter, carries with it an implied commitment that the Security Council or

---

[2]UNPROFOR was deployed in four sectors, designated East, West, North, and South. In April 1995, at Croatian insistence, the operation was renamed the United Nations Confidence Restoration Operation in Croatia (UNCRO). In May, the Croatian Army overran Sector West, and, in August, it overran Sectors North and South (Krajina), compelling Croatian Serbs to flee, and effectively ending UNCRO. Currently, the United Nations Transitional Administration for Eastern Slavonia, Baranja and Western Sirmium (UNTAES) is deployed in Sector East, the last Serb-held territory in Croatia. Yugoslavia has agreed in principle to return this area to Croatia.

member states acting on its behalf will respond with particular alacrity and severity in the event of violations.

Observation to Help Implement. In this subtype, the intention is to help implement agreements by assuring each party that other parties are in compliance or are making efforts to comply. There is no implied commitment that the Security Council will respond with particular alacrity and severity if the observers detect violations or even if they are expelled by the parties.

For example, the United Nations Good Offices Mission in Afghanistan and Pakistan (UNGOMAP) was charged with monitoring compliance with the 1988 Geneva Accords mediated by the United Nations and guaranteed in part by the Soviet Union and the United States. These accords included the withdrawal of Soviet troops from Afghanistan. UNGOMAP observers were drawn from established observer missions and were deployed in two-man teams.

Eager to demonstrate their compliance with the accords, the Soviets actively helped the observers to monitor aspects of their withdrawal. But the observers were not able to monitor non-intervention by other powers in Afghanistan or the return of refugees, because the country fell into civil war, making operations too difficult and risky for the observers.

Thus, UNGOMAP was partially successful in facilitating the Geneva Accords, primarily through assuring others that the Soviet Union was withdrawing its forces on schedule. By accepting the observers, the Soviet Union made its operations more transparent to the Security Council and gave an assurance of good faith. But if the Soviet Union had refused to comply with the Geneva Accords, there was no implied commitment for the Security Council to respond.

Observation to Deter. In this subtype, the intention is to deter violations by implying that the Security Council or member states will respond with particular alacrity and severity if violations occur.

For example, the United Nations Preventive Deployment Force (UNPREDEP) was deployed with the intent of deterring violations of Macedonia's northern border, building on a diplomatic warning delivered by the Bush Administration to Yugoslavia (Serbia and Montenegro). UNPREDEP covers the borders with Albania and Serbia, primarily by operating observation posts near crossing points. If violations occurred, perhaps as a result of Albanian-Serb conflict in Kosovo, the Security Council or member states acting on its behalf would, presumably, respond forcefully. If there were no forceful response, the operation would be exposed as a bluff.

The commonly used expression "preventive deployment" that appears in U.N. documents and the title UNPREDEP are misleading. The deployed force cannot *prevent* violations; it can only *report* that they have occurred. It can achieve deterrent effect as a marker or symbol of the Council's determination to respond with greater force if violations occur—not through its own strength.

Interposition

In this peace operation, the peace force is expected to control a buffer zone between the parties. *Control* implies that the force will detect violations and challenge those responsible, not that the force will defend the buffer zone against large-scale incursion. Interposition is more intrusive than observation, because the parties relinquish sovereign rights over the territory within the buffer zone. By relinquishing those rights, the parties allow their forces to disengage, diminishing the likelihood of confrontation; in some cases, the parties gain strategic warning of attack.

Control implies the ability to observe the buffer zone and to challenge unauthorized entry, but not to defend the entire zone. In some instances, the peace force has been authorized to defend itself in place; in such a situation, it may also be defending parts of the buffer zone. But to date, the peace force has usually been militarily insignificant when compared with the forces of the parties. Thus, controlling the buffer depended critically on the consent of the parties, not on the military capability of the peace force. In addition to controlling the buffer zone, the peace force has sometimes also monitored arms limitations outside the zone.

There are two subtypes of interposition mandate, each having different implications for decisionmakers. The first subtype is intended to help implement agreement among the parties. There is no implied commitment that the Security Council will respond in any particular way to incursion. The second subtype is intended to deter, with an implied commitment that the Security Council or member states acting on its behalf will respond with particular alacrity and severity in the event of incursion.

Interposition to Help Implement. In this subtype, the intention is to help implement agreements among the parties, particularly disengagement of forces and related arms limitations, by assuring each party that the other is complying or making efforts to comply. The onus to comply is on the parties.

The United Nations Disengagement Observer Force (UNDOF) is an example of deliberately planned interposition integral to an agreement. UNDOF is deployed in a buffer zone on the strategically important Golan Heights. Israel originally asked for a peace force large enough to offer significant resistance if Syria attacked, whereas Syria wanted just a small number of observers.

Had the Israeli position been adopted, UNDOF would have afforded an example of a militarily significant interposition force. But in a compromise, UNDOF was initially authorized 1,250 men, including two small infantry battalions, a force that would be insignificant in the event of an Israeli-Syrian war. UNDOF helped implement the 1974 Disengagement Agreement while holding open the possibility of a negotiated settlement of the Golan question.

The United Nations Peace-Keeping Force in Cyprus is an example of interposition initially conducted ad hoc during a conflict. Deployed in Cyprus during 1964, UNFICYP was placed in an extremely dangerous position by the Turkish intervention ten years later. Under the press of events, UNFICYP interposed itself between Turkish and Greek Cypriot forces, especially in the Nicosia area. UNFICYP subsequently helped to define the line of confrontation and occupied a buffer zone running the entire length of the island.

Over the past two decades, UNFICYP has declined to an authorized strength of 1,050 troops, just large enough to observe the buffer and to challenge small-scale violations. But the dominant military force in Cyprus is a Turkish corps protecting the Turkish Cypriots. The situation remains stable in a military sense, because Turkey has overwhelming force but no further territorial ambitions.

Interposition to Deter. In this subtype, the intention is to deter violations by implying that the Security Council or member states will respond with particular alacrity and severity if violations occur. As with observation to deter, the peace force normally has negligible military significance. Deterrence rests on the potential violator's expectation that the Council will respond, not on actions it anticipates the peace force might take.

The United Nations Iraq-Kuwait Observation Mission (UNIKOM) illustrates this type of operation. It has monitored a demilitarized zone on the border between Iraq and Kuwait since the Persian Gulf War. UNIKOM is not intended to help implement an agreement between Iraq and Kuwait. Rather, it is intended to deter Iraqi violations by demonstrating the will of the Security Council or member states acting on its behalf to maintain the sovereignty and independence of Kuwait.

During October 1994, the Iraqi dictator Saddam Hussein deployed heavy maneuver forces in a threatening fashion, eliciting a military response from the United States and several Persian Gulf states. The United States rapidly deployed attack aircraft to Kuwait and Saudi Arabia, strengthened its naval forces in the Persian Gulf, and deployed a small mechanized force in Kuwait. This response deterred Saddam Hussein, who subsequently withdrew his forces from positions threatening to Kuwait.

Deterrence depended upon this response, not upon any actions by UNIKOM, whose strength barely sufficed to keep the buffer zone under observation.

As with all U.N. forces, UNIKOM is in constant (24-hour-a-day) communication with U.N. headquarters in New York, through the Department of Peacekeeping Operations. However, because the United States has more-effective and -extensive intelligence collection than UNIKOM, the United States would probably detect an Iraqi threat before UNIKOM did.

Transition[3]

For a transition operation, the peace force is expected to assist the parties in changing the status or condition of a country. A transition operation can be extremely difficult and highly intrusive, even to the extent of placing a country or parts of a country under temporary governance by the United Nations. Transition requires a high degree of consent—not just acquiescence, but active cooperation in achieving the new status or condition.

The force may facilitate demobilization, arms limitations, referenda, national reconciliation, elections, and creation of new governmental forms. For example, the peace force may facilitate demobilization by establishing collection points, receiving and safeguarding arms, and protecting former soldiers during the process.

The Security Council has invoked both Chapter VI and Chapter VII for transition operations.

Transition Under Chapter VI. The Security Council has authorized transition operations under Chapter VI to facilitate transitions from colonial rule or trusteeship to independence and to help parties terminate civil conflict through some form of agreement. Invoking Chapter VI implies that the peace force will accept combat in self-defense while accomplishing the tasks contained in its mandate.

Transition to Independence. West New Guinea, Namibia, and Western Sahara illustrate peace operations intended to facilitate transitions to independence for areas formerly under colonial rule.

The United Nations Temporary Executive Authority/United Nations Security Force in West New Guinea (UNTEA/UNSF) oversaw transition from a Dutch colony to a province of Indonesia. President Sukarno, who led the Republic of Indonesia at the time, had a long record of opposing Dutch colonial rule. Almost all the territory of Indonesia had been part of the Netherlands East Indies until it was wrested from the Dutch by an Indonesian independence movement

---

[3]The U.N. uses *transition* in the sense used in this study. Examples are the United Nations Transitional Administration for Eastern Slavonia, Baranja and Western Sirmium (UNTAES), the United Nations Transitional Authority in Cambodia (UNTAC), and the United Nations Transition Assistance Group (UNTAG).

under Sukarno's leadership. He repeatedly brought the issue of western New Guinea, the last area held by the Dutch, before the General Assembly, knowing that Britain or France would block action by the Security Council. Finally, in 1960, he broke diplomatic relations with the Netherlands and began to prepare his forces to seize western New Guinea.

Already involved in Vietnam, the United States was anxious to avert war between its ally the Netherlands and Indonesia, an important regional power under anti-communist leadership. Warning both parties to resolve their differences through negotiation, the United States mediated secret negotiations. (Officially, the mediator, Ellsworth Bunker, represented the Secretary-General, but he also reflected the views of his own government.) In September 1962, Indonesia and the Netherlands announced agreement on a cease-fire, transfer of administration to the U.N., subsequent transfer of administration to Indonesia, and finally an expression of free choice by the people.

These agreements formed the mandate for UNTEA/UNSF, which served as a buffer between the departing Dutch and the arriving Indonesians. In spring 1963, UNTEA/UNSF terminated operations, leaving western New Guinea under Indonesian control. Several years later, Indonesian officials selected the representatives to a series of tribal councils that decided unanimously to remain in Indonesia. This proceeding was not a free choice, but war between Indonesia and the Netherlands would probably not have changed the outcome.

In Namibia, the Security Council conducted a peace operation that led to creation of a new member state in the U.N. The League of Nations had assumed responsibility for this former German colony under the mandate system, but South Africa occupied Namibia during WWII and refused to relinquish administration to the U.N. Beginning in the 1960s, South Africa fought an unconventional war against the South West African People's Organization (SWAPO). In 1975, the situation was complicated by the outbreak of civil war in Angola to the north. South Africa conducted repeated incursions into Angola to counter the Marxist government in Luanda, which was supported by Cuban troops. But by the mid-1980s, South Africa became tired of this protracted, inconclusive warfare; the Soviet Union lost interest in supporting the Luandan government; and Fidel Castro became eager to recover his troops.

These trends allowed the United States to mediate an agreement among Angola, Cuba, and South Africa in 1988 that linked Cuban withdrawal to Namibian independence. To help implement this agreement, the United Nations Transition Assistance Group in Namibia (UNTAG) was to monitor the cease-fire and to ensure the independence of Namibia through free elections. With only three infantry battalions, UNTAG could not militarily oppose any party to the agreement.

In April 1989, SWAPO forces entered Namibia from Angola and clashed with police, threatening to disrupt the peace process. In this emergency, UNTAG authorized South African forces to act on behalf of the U.N. in combating SWAPO—a highly unorthodox expedient that was successful. Thereafter, UNTAG troops, police monitors, and election monitors combined to supervise voter registration and elections to a Constituent Assembly that established an independent state of Namibia.

The United Nations Mission for the Referendum in Western Sahara (MINURSO) is supposed to oversee a referendum giving the inhabitants a choice between Morocco and the independence movement known as *Frente Popular para la Liberación de Saguia el-Hamra y de Rio de Oro* (POLISARIO). The former Spanish colony of Western Sahara is extremely poor, and its inhabitants are largely nomadic. In 1975, the International Court of Justice disallowed Morocco's historical claim. Immediately thereafter, King Hassan of Morocco ordered thousands of his subjects into Western Sahara to support his side. Following a secret agreement, Moroccan forces occupied the north and Mauritanian forces occupied the south. With help from Algeria and Libya, POLISARIO fought, guerrilla style, against the occupying troops. Mauritania withdrew its forces in 1979, but Morocco strengthened its hold by building a defensive line along the entire 3,000-kilometer length of the country.

African states generally supported POLISARIO, whereas France and the United States tended to favor Morocco. In 1988, Morocco and POLISARIO agreed to a peace plan proposed jointly by the United Nations and the Organization of African Unity (OAU). As subsequently modified, the peace plan foresaw a cease-fire, reduction of Moroccan troops, voter registration, and a referendum to determine the status of Western Sahara. The cease-fire of September 1991 is still holding; otherwise, there has been little progress. Morocco is determined to produce a voter registration that guarantees a result favorable to its side. In the meantime, POLISARIO has slowly declined as it loses its patrons.

Termination of Civil Conflict. A common transition is national reconciliation or some other agreement ending civil conflict. The country in question may change its constitution or be newly constituted. The process normally begins with a cease-fire and includes demobilization and disarmament. It may include reforming police and military forces, holding national elections, and reconstructing damaged infrastructure. Operations in Cyprus, Nicaragua, Mozambique, Cambodia, and Croatia provide examples.

The Secretary-General initially assumed that the United Nations Peace-Keeping Force in Cyprus would assist Greek Cypriots and Turkish Cypriots in returning to normal conditions, because he presumed that the two parties would be willing to cooperate in some kind of central government. Originally authorized 7,000 troops, UNFICYP was too small to enforce its will on the communities in Cyprus, much less their patrons, nor was such a role ever contemplated. UNFICYP made modest progress in allaying tensions on the island, but it could not bring the parties to cooperate. The Turkish Cypriots were unwilling to accept minority status in a central government, and the Turkish intervention in 1974 caused a de facto partition of the island along national lines, which appears to be permanent.

In Nicaragua, the United Nations Observer Group in Central America (ONUCA), augmented by an infantry battalion, successfully conducted voluntary demobilization of the Contras, an insurgent organization that had fought the Sandinistas from bases in Honduras with support from the United States. The Contra leaders were willing to demobilize because they had lost external support and were no longer welcome in Honduras. Moreover, their enemies, the Sandinistas, lost the presidential election in Nicaragua. Even so, the Contra leaders remained deeply suspicious of the Sandinistas and demobilization proceeded slowly. By the end of the operation, approximately 22,000 Contra guerrillas turned over weapons in their possession and received demobilization certificates plus an issue of food and clothing. While ONUCA undoubtedly helped implement agreements, the continuing interest and pressure of regional governments drove the peace process.

ONUMOZ was mandated to monitor the cease-fire between the parties, the separation of their forces, and demobilization, including the collection of weapons and the eventual destruction of those weapons. It was to monitor disbanding of irregular forces, provide security for vital installations, and coordinate humanitarian assistance. After many setbacks, this operation ended successfully.

The United Nations Transitional Authority in Cambodia (UNTAC) was expected to help implement voluntary demobilization by regrouping forces of the warring parties and taking custody of weapons in cantonment areas. UNTAC included 12 infantry battalions, a force too small to confront either of the major parties. Moreover, the contributing member states would not have supported any combat beyond strictly defined self-defense. The Party of Democratic Kampuchea (PDK), otherwise known as the Pol Pot faction of the Khmer Rouge, refused to allow freedom of movement to UNTAC in the areas it controlled. Alleging that other parties had violated the Paris Agreement of October 23, 1991, the PDK withdrew from the peace process, despite repeated efforts by UNTAC to negotiate a compromise.

For its part, the Cambodian government, largely composed of Khmer Rouge disaffected with Pol Pot, refused to allow UNTAC observers into its areas of operations against the PDK. As a result, UNTAC was unable to demobilize the PDK or large elements of Cambodian government forces, although it did demobilize two smaller militias.

UNTAC successfully oversaw a national election in June 1993, which resulted in a victory for the United Front for an Independent, Neutral, and Cooperative Cambodia (FUNCINPEC), a moderate Royalist party loyal to Prince Sihanouk. The new government has so far successfully defended itself against the PDK.

In Croatia, the Security Council approved an open-ended transition mandate that presupposed no particular kind of settlement. It stated that the United Nations Protection Force "should be an interim arrangement to create conditions of peace and security required for negotiation of an overall settlement of the Yugoslav crisis."[4] To this end, UNPROFOR assumed responsibility for United Nations Protected Areas (UNPAs), in which militias would be disarmed and persons would be protected from armed attack. These UNPAs and the adjacent "pink zones"[5] represented roughly the Serb-held areas of Croatia. UNPROFOR deployed 12 infantry battalions into the UNPAs, including units from the great powers France and Russia. These forces were too small to undertake successful combat operations against regular Croatian forces or Serb militias, and UNPROFOR had no authority to use force except in self-defense. UNPROFOR depended on consent of the parties to accomplish its mandate, but both Croatia and the Croatian Serbs refused to cooperate. Croatian Serbs carried out "ethnic cleansing"[6] against non-Serbs in Krajina; the non-Serbs became refugees in Croatia. On several occasions, Croatia attacked the Croatian Serbs, compelling them to recover their heavy weapons from collection points and ending attempts at disarmament.

In April 1995, the operation was renamed the United Nations Confidence Restoration Operation in Croatia and was required to monitor the border between Croatia and Bosnia-Herzegovina. On May 3, 1995, Croatia seized an UNPA (Sector West), and UNCRO helped Serbs to flee. On August 4, 1995, the Croatian Army overran two UNPAs (Sectors North and South, comprising Krajina), killing three U.N. soldiers and driving away most of the Serb population.

Transition Operation Under Chapter VII. In two civil conflicts— UNOSOM II in cooperation with U.S. forces, and UNPROFOR in Bosnia-Herzegovina in cooperation with NATO forces—the Security Council authorized transition operations under Chapter VII. Those operations eventually turned into attempts at peace enforcement. Both attempts failed catastrophically because the peace force on the

---

[4]Security Council Resolution 743, February 2, 1992.

[5]"Pink zones" were Serb-held areas outside the formal borders of UNPAs; in some instances, they were gained by force after the UNPAs were delineated.

[6]The odious expression "ethnic cleansing" is a euphemism for forcing civilians from their homes, often through intimidation, beatings, arson, and murder.

ground was neither equipped for combat operations nor appropriately controlled.

Another transition operation under Chapter VII did not require enforcement: the Multinational Force in Haiti (Restore Democracy). In this case, the Cédras regime acquiesced to its own demise, because it was confronted by overwhelming force. In strong contrast to Somalia and Bosnia-Herzegovina, the peace force (almost entirely U.S.) was well prepared for combat operations and was controlled by a great power acting under authority of the Council.

Security for Humanitarian Aid[7]

In this type of operation, the peace force is expected to secure humanitarian aid that alleviates suffering caused by conflict.[8] The Force Commander's primary task is to *secure* aid, not to *provide* it, although he may also assist in providing it. Parties consent by agreeing not to obstruct humanitarian aid and to respect the force that secures it. Security for humanitarian aid typically includes securing transportation centers, lines of communication, and vital facilities such as power-generating plants, potable-water tanks, and storage capacity.

This type of operation extends only to humanitarian aid. Securing populations in safe areas would exceed its bounds and would imply a transition operation. Providing security to populations is the fundamental responsibility of a sovereign. The Security Council cannot assume such responsibility indefinitely, unless it creates an interminable trusteeship; therefore, it must look to an inevitable transition, e.g., resumption of power by a legitimate government, assumption of power by some newly created authority. In addition,

---

[7]"A second qualitative change is the use of United Nations forces to protect humanitarian operations. Humanitarian agencies endeavor to provide succour to civilian victims of war wherever they may be. Too often the warring parties make it difficult or impossible for them to do so. This is sometimes because of the exigencies of war but more often because the relief of a particular population is contrary to the war aims of one or other of the parties." Boutros-Ghali, *Agenda for Peace—1995*, 1995, Paragraph 18.

[8]The Security Council might also authorize this type of operation if a natural disaster were accompanied by wide-scale disorder and lawlessness without discernible parties.

it is usually impossible to secure populations without becoming deeply involved in the conflict (as demonstrated in Croatia and Bosnia-Herzegovina), because control over populations is a primary aim of belligerents.

Security for aid goes beyond self-defense of the force; therefore, the Security Council should, ideally, invoke Chapter VII. But on several occasions the Security Council has invoked Chapter VI for this type of operation: the United Nations Interim Force in Lebanon (UNIFIL), the First United Nations Operation in Somalia (UNOSOM I), and UNAMIR.[9]

UNIFIL is an extremely ill-defined operation[10] that eventually evolved, for lack of something better, into an operation to secure humanitarian aid. During the 1970s, Lebanon was fragmented into areas controlled by the Christian Phalange, the Muslim Amal, the Druze, the Palestine Liberation Organization (PLO), and Hezbollah, a radical Muslim group. In March 1978, Israel invaded southern Lebanon to suppress PLO attacks on Israeli civilians. In response, the United States sponsored a Security Council Resolution calling for a cease-fire in Lebanon, withdrawal of Israeli forces, and introduction of a peace force to reaffirm Lebanon's sovereign independence.

In June, Syrian forces invaded Lebanon with the tacit understanding that Syria would stop north of the "red line," roughly the Litani River. UNIFIL originally deployed seven infantry battalions authorized to use force in self-defense. They oversaw the Israeli withdrawal, but Israel relinquished control not to UNIFIL but to a friendly Lebanese militia. After Israel withdrew, it repeatedly entered Lebanon in pursuit of PLO guerrillas. In June 1982, Israel invaded Lebanon all the way to Beirut, leading to expulsion of the PLO, and subsequently created a security zone in southern Lebanon that overlapped the UNIFIL area of operations. During this invasion, Israeli forces brushed UNIFIL aside. Formally speaking, UNIFIL still has a transition mandate (eventual restoration of Lebanese government authority); in actuality, it only secures and provides humanitarian aid to the population.

---

[9]Research for this project was completed while UNAMIR was still in progress.

[10]The difficulty of discerning where UNIFIL fits in a typology suggests not that typologies are futile but that this operation lacked a clear, workable mandate.

In Somalia, UNOSOM I was to monitor a cease-fire and to secure humanitarian aid with 500 troops, later increased to 3,500. But before much reinforcement had arrived, the United States undertook a much larger operation (Restore Hope) to secure humanitarian aid through the Unified Task Force (UNITAF). UNITAF's mission (*mandate* in U.N. terms) was formulated as security for humanitarian aid:

> When directed by the [National Command Authority], CINCCENT will conduct joint and combined military operations in Somalia, to secure the major air and seaports, key installations and food distribution points, to provide open and free passage of relief supplies, to provide security for convoys and relief organization operations and assist UN/NGOs in providing humanitarian relief under UN auspices.[11]

However, during the conduct of operations, UNITAF responded to requests from U.N. officials and to exigencies in Somalia by accomplishing some disarmament as well. According to the Commander in Chief of the Central Command (USCINCCENT),

> great care was taken to develop an approved, well-defined mission with attainable, measurable objectives prior to the operation commencing. Disarmament was excluded from the mission because it was neither realistically achievable nor a prerequisite for the core mission of providing a secure environment for relief operations. Selective "disarming as necessary" became an implied task which led to the cantonment of heavy weapons and gave UNITAF the ability to conduct weapons sweeps.[12]

Acting under Chapter VII, UNITAF accomplished some disarmament, including house-to-house searches for illegal weapons. These actions addressed a fundamental cause of humanitarian disaster in Somalia: large quantities of military weapons in the possession of rival clans. But anxious to avoid deeper involvement, UNITAF left much disarmament for the less powerful UNOSOM II to accomplish. When the party led by Mohammed Farah Aideed attacked UNOSOM

---

[11]Waldo D. Freeman, Robert B. Lambert, and Jason D. Mims, "Operation Restore Hope: A USCENTCOM Perspective," *Military Review*, September 1993, p. 64.

[12]Joseph P. Hoar, "A CINC's Perspective," *JFQ Forum*, Autumn 1993, p. 58.

II, U.S. forces controlled unilaterally and UNOSOM II attempted peace enforcement.

UNITAF shows how consent may be affected by the military power of the peace force. In most peace operations, consent was affected by the countervailing forces of opposing parties and, very often, by diplomatic pressure, especially pressure exerted by great powers. But consent was not affected by the military power of the peace force because it was insignificant compared with that of the parties' forces. In strong contrast, UNITAF arrived in Somalia with an overwhelming force from the perspective of the rival clan leaders.

Mohammed Farah Aideed felt compelled by UNITAF capabilities and its liberal rules of engagement to maintain a grudging consent, which he withdrew after most UNITAF forces had left the country—a withdrawal of consent that was anticipated by Secretary-General Boutros-Ghali. Such withdrawal is the basis for the next type of peace operation: peace enforcement.

Peace Enforcement

In this type of operation, the peace force is expected to coerce recalcitrant parties into complying with their agreements or with resolutions of the Security Council. Normally, peace enforcement occurs in the context of an operation under Chapter VII, when a party or parties withdraw consent and the Security Council decides to enforce its will.

The critical decision is *whether* to invoke Chapter VII, not whether to attempt peace enforcement after invoking it. Chapter VII implies willingness to coerce parties if they withdraw consent, putting the initiative in the parties' hands. The worst failures in peace operations (Somalia and Bosnia-Herzegovina) occurred because the Security Council invoked Chapter VII without being prepared to coerce parties. On the contrary, displays of weakness encouraged parties to believe that they could defy the Security Council successfully.

There is a large practical difference between *peace enforcement,* which presumes impartiality, and *enforcement against a uniquely identified aggressor:* During peace enforcement, the Security Council precludes itself from allying with any party. To take a recent exam-

LIBRARY
COLBY-SAWYER COLLEGE
NEW LONDON, NH 03257

ple, the Security Council was impartial during the conflict in Bosnia-Herzegovina; therefore, UNPROFOR was not allowed to ally with the Muslim side. UNPROFOR was not permitted to advise, train, equip, or otherwise assist the Muslim side while NATO–UNPROFOR was trying to lift the siege of Sarajevo. During enforcement, the Security Council has allied with the victim of aggression. For example, the United Nations Command in Korea included (and would include again in wartime) South Korean forces. It was entirely permissible, indeed, essential, to increase the combat power of the forces of the Republic of Korea.

Congo. In 1960, the sudden end of Belgian rule left the Congo unprepared for independence. Alarmed that the Soviet Union might extend its influence into central Africa, the United States supported a transition operation to oversee the withdrawal of Belgian troops and to assist the legitimate government in extending its authority. That government appealed to the United Nations for help, forming the initial basis for consent. But it soon divided into factions led by President Joseph Kasavubu and Prime Minister Patrice Lumumba. In addition, Katanga Province, backed by mining interests, seceded from the Congo.

The Security Council eventually authorized ONUC to use force to avert civil war and to apprehend mercenaries. At its peak, ONUC mustered 19,550 personnel, largely light infantry deployed in widely scattered locations. The largest combat unit was an Indian infantry brigade that eventually restored Katanga Province to the Congo.

Somalia. In May 1993, UNOSOM II assumed control over peace operations in Somalia. It had Chapter VII authorization to use force and a mandate to facilitate national reconciliation of the warring parties as agreed in Addis Ababa—a process that included disarmament of the parties through collection of weapons, establishment of a national police force, and creation of new organs of government. The United States supported this operation with a battalion-sized quick-reaction force and special-operations forces under national control.

One month after UNOSOM II assumed control, forces commanded by Mohammed Farah Aideed attacked Pakistani forces. As foreseen by the Secretary-General, Aideed withdrew his consent to the peace process, especially to disarmament, as soon as the formidable UNITAF left Somalia. The Security Council responded by reaffirming that the Secretary-General was authorized to take "all necessary measures" against those responsible for the attacks and by urging members to contribute heavy forces and attack helicopters. U.S. special-operations forces attempted to apprehend Aideed but suffered casualties that caused the United States to withdraw.[13]

Bosnia-Herzegovina. UNPROFOR began operations in Bosnia when it deployed its headquarters to Sarajevo in March 1992, expecting that its presence would have a calming effect. In April, the Bosnian Serbs began a siege of Sarajevo, forcing UNPROFOR to relocate its headquarters to Zagreb. In June, UNPROFOR returned to Sarajevo to implement an agreement among the parties and UNPROFOR, opening the airport for humanitarian aid. Neither of the parties kept that agreement, but UNPROFOR succeeded in operating the airport despite occasional gunfire. In May 1993, the Security Council, acting under Chapter VII, declared six safe areas. The Force Commander estimated that 34,000 additional troops would be required to deter attacks on safe areas, but agreed to attempt the operation with only 7,600 additional troops plus air support from NATO.

By enlarging the mandate to include safe areas, the Security Council went far beyond securing humanitarian aid. In fact, the safe areas were designed to perpetuate control by the Muslim-dominated government over areas of predominantly Muslim populations.

However, it soon became apparent that the ground-combat power of UNPROFOR was too weak to safely request close air support. In fact, units in outlying safe areas were virtually hostages to the Bosnian

---

[13]There is little evidence to support assertions that mission creep led to disaster in Somalia. In the sense intended by critics, "mission creep" means incremental extension of a mandate until a force is dangerously overtaxed. The United States extended the Unified Task Force (UNITAF) mandate to include some disarmament of the factions, but not to the extent of overtaxing this highly capable force. The Security Council gave UNOSOM II an ambitious mandate, including disarmament of the factions. Arguably, this less-capable force was overtaxed from the outset by its mandate. Mohammed Farah Aideed promptly attacked UNOSOM II troops, causing the Security Council to make a deliberate, explicit decision to bring him to account. In retrospect, the United States should either have accepted a more-ambitious transition mandate for UNITAF or should have insisted that operations in Somalia terminate with the departure of UNITAF.

Serbs. In March–April 1994, the Bosnian Serbs attacked the Gorazde safe area, eventually prompting NATO to issue an ultimatum. In November, they attacked the Bihac safe area, this time provoking little response. In July 1995, they overran the safe areas of Srebrenica and Zepa and perpetrated mass atrocities.

In February 1994, an explosion in the produce market of Sarajevo killed 68 persons, prompting NATO to issue an ultimatum to the parties. NATO threatened to conduct air strikes on heavy weapons found within an exclusion zone (a zone in which no heavy weapons were allowed) 12 miles from the center of Sarajevo. UNPROFOR undertook to operate collection points for heavy weapons remaining within the exclusion zone. The Bosnian Serbs complied with this ultimatum, ending the bombardment of Sarajevo.

NATO's role was unequivocally peace enforcement, but UNPROFOR's role was ambiguous or confused. Although the Security Council repeatedly invoked Chapter VII, UNPROFOR remained configured for Chapter VI operations, a gross mismatch of force and mandate. Out of weakness, it was compelled to proclaim itself a "peace-keeping" force operating with consent, even when assisting NATO in the enforcement of exclusion zones. Quite understandably, the Bosnian Serbs regarded UNPROFOR as a belligerent.

During a crisis in May 1995, Bosnian Serbs took hundreds of UNPROFOR personnel hostage, chaining some to critical facilities to deter NATO air strikes. The weapon-collection points around Sarajevo were dissolved, and the Serbs renewed their bombardment of the city. In August 1995, another great loss of civilian life prompted an extensive NATO air operation that eventually lifted the siege of Sarajevo. (Although effective, the air campaign probably had less effect on Serb attitudes than did the successful Croatian offensives in late 1995, especially the recapture of Krajina.) During the air operation, UNPROFOR was deployed only in Muslim-held territory, thus reducing its vulnerability to retaliation.

The Dayton Agreements in November 1995 foresaw creation of an Implementation Force equipped for combat operations and controlled by NATO: a force configured for Chapter VII—at last correlating the peace force with its mandate.

ENFORCEMENT

A force acting under authority of the Security Council is expected to restore international peace and security by conducting combat operations against a uniquely identified aggressor. There is no requirement for impartiality or consent; therefore, *enforcement* falls outside the definition of *peace operations.*

Chapter VII of the Charter of the United Nations contains provisions for military action, but member states have not implemented key articles of Chapter VII. They have not agreed to put forces on call (Article 43), to hold air forces immediately available for combined action (Article 45), or to establish a Military Staff Committee (Article 47) as envisioned. As a result, the Security Council has not attempted to conduct enforcement through the U.N. However, in two cases it has authorized member states to do so.

Korea

In 1950, the Security Council made the United States its executive agent to repel invasion of South Korea by the Communist government of North Korea. This action was possible because the ambassador from the Soviet Union was absent. The senior U.S. commander in Korea at that time, General Douglas MacArthur, became simultaneously the Commander in Chief, United Nations Command (CINCUNC), an arrangement that has endured to the present. CINCUNC reports to the National Command Authority of the United States, not to the Security Council. No forces are currently assigned to CINCUNC other than a small security force in the conference area located in the demilitarized zone. But in the event of war in the Korean peninsula, CINCUNC would assume command of any forces contributed by member states.

Kuwait

On November 29, 1990, the Security Council passed Resolution 678, demanding that Iraq withdraw its forces from Kuwait and authorizing member states "to use all necessary means" to this end. The member states formed a coalition. Command arrangements centered on the United States and Saudi Arabia, the leading members of this coalition. USCINCCENT commanded U.S. forces and controlled other Western forces. Joint Forces Command, headed by a Saudi general, commanded Saudi forces and controlled other Arab and Islamic forces. Security Council Resolution 678 merely requested member states "to keep the Council regularly informed on the progress of actions."

OVERVIEW OF AN OPERATIONAL TYPOLOGY

This section summarizes types of peace operations discussed in the preceding sections, for ease of reference.

Diplomacy–Peace Operations–Enforcement

Actions that the United Nations takes or authorizes member states to take for maintaining or restoring international peace and security are summarized in Figure 3.1. Each action is characterized by the chapter in the Charter of the United Nations, the consent required from the parties to a conflict (also referred to as "required consent"), and the broadly defined mandate.

Diplomacy includes the actions contemplated in Article 33, i.e., negotiation, inquiry, mediation, conciliation, arbitration, judicial settlement, resort to regional agencies, and "other peaceful means." It may also include acceptance of a peace operation whose mandate may be shaped by agreements, often reached through the mediation or good offices of the United Nations or powers acting on its behalf.

The types of peace operations are ordered by intrusiveness[14]—not by the prevalence of conflict—beginning with observation, the least

---

[14]This order is obvious except for transition operations and security for humanitarian aid. Transition operations are more comprehensive, but their intrusiveness varies. At one extreme, especially when conducted under Chapter VII, transition operations can be exceedingly intrusive, far more so than measures that would be required to secure humanitarian aid. Indeed, security for humanitarian aid could be included within a larger transition operation. At the other extreme, transition operations can be much less intrusive, little more than a service provided to the parties. In any case, security for humanitarian aid implies willingness to use force beyond self-defense, an intrusion of considerable importance, and humanitarian aid may have consequences affecting the course of conflict.

RAND*MR582-3.1*

	Diplomacy	Peace Operations: Security Council does not take sides.					Enforcement: Security Council sides with the victim against the aggressor.
		Peace-Keeping		More-Ambitious Operations			
		Observation	Interposition	Transition	Security for Humanitarian Aid	Peace Enforcement	
Chapter of the U.N. Charter		Chapter VI		Chapter VI or Chapter VII		Chapter VII	
Consent Required from the Parties	Accept a peace operation	Allow access to observers	Acquiesce in impartial control of a buffer zone	Cooperate in achieving new condition and status	Allow provision of aid	None: occurs when party *withdraws* consent	Not required
Typical Mandate	Negotiate mandate for a peace operation	Observe compliance with agreements; report violations; mediate among parties	Create buffer zones; control entry into buffer zones; monitor arms limitations	Provide secure conditions; oversee demobilization; secure electoral activities; facilitate reconstruction	Provide security for humanitarian aid	Coerce recalcitrant parties into complying with UNSC resolutions or their agreements	Enforce sanctions; conduct other military operations to maintain or to restore peace and security

Figure 3.1—Diplomacy–Peace Operations–Enforcement

intrusive, and ascending to peace enforcement, which implies combat operations. Observation might occur during a precarious cease-fire, for example, UNIIMOG (Iran-Iraq), or in an almost completely peaceful setting, for example, UNPROFOR in Macedonia up to spring 1996. Similarly, a transition operation might occur in a relatively peaceful situation, for example, UNTEA/UNSF (western New Guinea), or during a violent conflict, for example, UNPROFOR in Croatia. An operational typology focuses on what the force is expected to accomplish, so the result is a spectrum of types of operations, not a spectrum of conflict.

To assess how much consent will be expected from the parties, what capabilities the peace force will need, what support will be required from member states, etc., a given operation should be defined by its high end. Within each type of operation, a peace force will often be expected to perform less-intrusive actions. For example, observation is often subsumed in other types of peace operations.

Ultimately, success or failure will be judged by the most intrusive aspect of the operation. For example, UNPROFOR, operating in coordination with NATO in Bosnia-Herzegovina, usually failed at peace enforcement, the most intrusive part of its mandate. This failure, epitomized by the Srebrenica debacle, eclipsed UNPROFOR's modest accomplishments in lesser operations, including security for humanitarian aid.

Assessment of responsibility is the fundamental difference between peace enforcement and enforcement. In peace enforcement, as in all peace operations, the Security Council holds that parties share responsibility and therefore is impartial among them. Conversely, the Council may undertake enforcement when it believes there is a unique aggressor. In such a circumstance, the Security Council holds the aggressor responsible, not its victim. In 1950, for example, the Security Council (less the Soviet Union) held that the Democratic People's Republic of Korea (North Korea) had attacked without provocation and that the Republic of Korea (South Korea) was blameless. It consequently sided with the victim against the aggressor.

Peace Operations and Their Variants

Peace operations, including variants of the basic types, are summarized in Figure 3.2.

Observation and interposition have variants defined by the intent of the Security Council. These operations may be intended to help implement agreements or they may be intended to deter violations, in which case, response to violations becomes crucial. This response may be articulated in the mandate or in related communications by the Secretary-General or member states acting on behalf of the United Nations. For example, the deterrent effect of UNPREDEP in Macedonia is related to a diplomatic exchange between the United States and Yugoslavia (Serbia and Montenegro).

Transition and security operations also have variants, defined by whether they invoke Chapter VI or Chapter VII. The Security Council usually invokes Chapter VI when it believes that consent is robust, the parties firmly control their supporters, and no other groups

RAND*MR582-3.2*

Peace Operations							
Peace-Keeping				More-Ambitious Operations			
Observation		Interposition		Transition		Security for Humanitarian Aid	Peace Enforcement
Facilitate agreement	Deter violations	Facilitate agreement	Deter violations				
Chapter of the U.N. Charter	Chapter VI (self-defense)			Chapter VI (self-defense)	Chapter VII (potential enforcement)	Chapter VII (secure aid)	Chapter VII (enforce will of UNSC)
Consent Required from the Parties	Allow access to observers		Acquiesce in impartial control of a buffer zone		Cooperate in achieving new condition and status of a country	Allow provision of aid	None: occurs when party *withdraws* consent
Typical Mandate	Observe compliance with agreements; report violations; mediate among parties	Plus respond forcefully to violations	Create buffer zones; control entry into buffer zones; monitor arms limitations	Plus respond forcefully to violations	Provide secure conditions; oversee demobilization, demilitarization, arms limitations; provide security for electoral activities; facilitate reconstruction; cooperate closely with civilian component and NGOs		Provide security for humanitarian aid	Coerce recalcitrant parties into complying with UNSC resolutions and parties' agreements

|◄──────────── Chapter VI ────────────►|◄──────── Chapter VII ────────►|

Figure 3.2—Peace Operations and Their Variants

threaten to disrupt the operation. The peace force is authorized to employ force only in self-defense while accomplishing the mandate, not to coerce any party into compliance. Conversely, the Security Council usually invokes Chapter VII when it believes that consent is fragile, the parties do not firmly control their supporters, or other groups threaten to disrupt the operation. The peace force is authorized to coerce parties into complying with agreements and to use force against other groups that threaten to disrupt the operation.

Military requirements for any operation under Chapter VII, even security for humanitarian aid, may be identical to requirements for peace enforcement. Requirements are identical when the Security Council believes consent is so fragile that the peace force must be constantly ready to enforce its will. Requirements may not be identical when the Security Council believes that consent is robust and can be maintained without initially deploying an overwhelming force. But even in such cases, invoking Chapter VII implies that the Security

Council must be prepared to deploy an overwhelming force if challenged or else suffer loss of prestige.

Peace enforcement raises critical issues that must be addressed if the operation is to have a good prospect for success:

- The Permanent Five must form a robust consensus, and one or more of the Permanent Five will likely have to contribute forces.

- The contributors must believe that their interests justify combat operations and that domestic constituencies will tolerate casualties associated with combat.

- The capabilities, control during combat, and appearance of the peace force must be appropriate. It is absurd and dangerous for troops to attempt peace enforcement while making themselves conspicuous by wearing blue helmets and driving white-painted vehicles,[15] as UNOSOM II in Somalia and UNPROFOR in Bosnia-Herzegovina demonstrated.

Historical and Current Peace Operations Classified by Type

To demonstrate utility, selected peace operations are classified in Figure 3.3 according to an operational typology. The result illustrates the changing character of particular peace operations, such as the United Nations Observer Group in Central America and the United Nations Peace-Keeping Force in Cyprus,[16] and the trend to more-ambitious operations in recent years.

Despite its name, the United Nations Iraq-Kuwait Observer Mission (UNIKOM) has an interposition mandate to control a buffer zone on

---

[15]Of course, being camouflaged does not guarantee successful peace enforcement if the peace force lacks required capabilities. For example, U.S. forces that supported UNOSOM II in Somalia did not wear blue helmets or operate white vehicles; the operation failed because the United States did not have enough interest in Somalia to either send the required heavy forces or to sustain casualties suffered by light forces operating at high risk to themselves.

[16]These were chosen to illustrate changes from one type of operation to another. If all such changes were shown, the figure would become cluttered. For example, the operations under "peace enforcement" began as transition operations.

RAND*MR582-3.3*

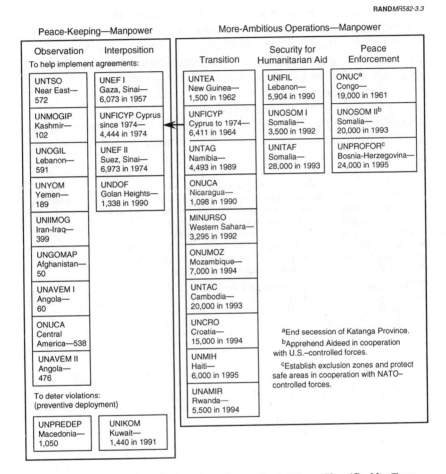

Figure 3.3—Historical and Current Peace Operations Classified by Type

the Iraq-Kuwait border. The United Nations Interim Force in Lebanon (UNIFIL) originally had an unworkable transition mandate that devolved into an attempt to secure humanitarian aid for the civilian population. Until 1974, UNFICYP attempted to accomplish a transition mandate. After the Turkish intervention, UNFICYP assumed an interposition mandate, controlling a buffer zone between the two communities on Cyprus.

A United Nations Peace Force (UNPF) conducted different types of operations in three republics of the former Yugoslavia.[17] In Croatia, UNPROFOR (later UNCRO) originally had a transition mandate. But in 1994, that mandate shifted to an interposition mandate for controlling a buffer zone between Croatian forces and Serbs in Krajina.[18] In Bosnia-Herzegovina, UNPROFOR, in coordination with NATO, attempted peace enforcement of exclusion zones and safe areas. In Macedonia, UNPREDEP still accomplishes an observation mandate with an intention to deter violations of the northern border.

---

[17]On March 31, 1995, the Security Council renamed control entities in the former Yugoslavia to reflect their various characters. Control over all U.N. forces was vested in the United Nations Peace Force (UNPF), with headquarters in Zagreb. In Croatia, the United Nations Confidence Restoration Operation in Croatia (UNCRO) exercised control. (Croatian officials insisted on the qualifying phrase "in Croatia," but it was not reflected in the official abbreviation.) In Bosnia-Herzegovina, UNPROFOR (originally the name for all U.N. forces) exercised control. In Macedonia, the United Nations Preventive Deployment Force (UNPREDEP) exercised control.

[18]During August 4–7, 1995, Croatian forces overran Krajina. By Resolution 1037 on January 15, 1996, the Security Council established the United Nations Transitional Administration for Eastern Slavonia, Baranja and Western Sirmium (UNTAES) in the last Serb-held area of Croatia.

Chapter Four

EVALUATING PEACE OPERATIONS

This chapter provides a first-order evaluation[1] of success and failure in peace operations across the spectrum.

FULFILLING THE MANDATE

From an operational perspective, *success* means fulfilling the mandate. The operation should be considered successful when it accomplishes the tasks implied by the mandate, even when conflict resumes for reasons beyond the control of the peace force. If, on the other hand, the peace force does not fulfill the mandate, either because it lacks required capabilities or because the parties refuse to cooperate, the operation should be considered a failure, whatever happens in the conflict.

To assume that an operation succeeded because the conflict subsided is to fall into a *post hoc, ergo propter hoc* fallacy. Almost every conflict will subside sooner or later, largely from its own dynamics, whether or not there is any peace operation. Moreover, most peace operations are not coercive. They are intended to facilitate a process that parties agree to accomplish—not to coerce the parties—and therefore volition of the parties weighs more heavily than actions of the peace force. Even peace enforcement, decisive as it may be at the time, is only a temporary expedient.

---

[1]Thus, it answers the first question posed in Chapter One (whether the operation itself was successful). Answering the second question (how much its success contributed to resolving the conflict) would require a complex and highly detailed analysis, exceeding the bounds of this report.

PEACE-KEEPING

Observation

Observation has a mixed record of success and failure. This type of operation helped to implement viable agreements, but it failed quickly when the parties renewed hostilities or preferred to evade scrutiny. In addition, observers often encountered rugged terrain, inadequate equipment, and the prevalence of unconventional warfare. Figure 4.1 evaluates cases of observation.

The United Nations Truce Supervision Organization (UNTSO) could not monitor compliance with the 1949 armistices between Israel and

RAND*MR582-4.1*

Operation— Manpower	Mandate	Fulfilled?
UNTSO (Near East)—572	Monitor compliance with 1949 armistices between Israel and Egypt, Jordan, Lebanon, Syria.	No
UNMOGIP (Kashmir)—102	Monitor compliance with the Karachi Agreement of 1949 between India and Pakistan.	Yes to 1971; no since
UNOGIL (Lebanon)—591	Ensure that there is no illegal infiltration of personnel and arms into Lebanon.	No
UNYOM (Yemen)—189	Verify withdrawal of Egyptian troops and cessation of Saudi aid to Royalist faction.	No
UNIIMOG (Iran-Iraq)—399	Verify, confirm, and supervise the 1988 cease-fire between Iran and Iraq.	Partially
UNGOMAP (Afghanistan)—50	Verify implementation of the 1988 Geneva Accords, including, among other things, withdrawal of Soviet forces.	Partially
UNAVEM I (Angola)—60	Verify phased withdrawal of Cuban forces from Angola.	Yes
ONUCA (Central America)—538	Monitor compliance with 1987 Esquipulas II Agreements regarding support to irregular forces.	No
UNAVEM II (Angola)—476	Verify arrangements by Angolan government and UNITA to monitor the 1991 cease-fire and police activities.	No
UNPROFOR[a] (Macedonia)—1,050	Observe activity on northern border of Macedonia; promote stability by presence (preventive deployment).	Yes

[a]Redesignated United Nations Preventive Deployment Force (UNPREDEP) in 1995.

Figure 4.1—Evaluating Observation Operations

its antagonists Egypt, Jordan, Lebanon, and Syria, initially because Israel and the Arab states refused to attend meetings of the Mixed Armistice Commissions after 1951 and, eventually, because hostilities obviated the agreements.

UNMOGIP initially helped to implement the Karachi Agreement of 1949 between India and Pakistan, but ultimately failed because India ceased to cooperate after 1971, when it launched a counterinsurgency campaign in Kashmir. Although India thus withdrew its consent, UNMOGIP still remained deployed to demonstrate continuing concern. A change in Indian policy toward Kashmir could make the operation viable again.

UNOGIL was too small and inadequately equipped to observe the borders between Lebanon and neighboring Israel and Syria. In addition, the Lebanese government did not control its own territory and could not guarantee the security of the observers. Despite its failure, UNOGIL advanced U.S. interests by giving political cover for withdrawal of U.S. forces from Lebanon.

UNYOM was too small and inadequately supplied with aircraft to observe the northwestern border of Yemen and thus verify the withdrawal of Egyptian troops or cessation of Saudi aid to the Royalists. Moreover, Egypt and Saudi Arabia were not committed to peace, despite signing an agreement at American insistence. When UNYOM terminated operations in 1964, Egypt was still sending reinforcements to Yemen.

UNIIMOG was frustrated by Iran's refusal to cooperate fully and by lack of aircraft to monitor the 1,400-kilometer-long border between the two countries. UNIIMOG withdrew when Coalition ground forces went on the offensive against Iraq during the Persian Gulf War.

UNGOMAP was able to observe the Soviet withdrawal from Afghanistan, because the Soviets wanted to leave the country and to have their departure confirmed. But UNGOMAP could not verify non-interference by neighboring powers or assist refugees because it could not cover the area of interest and because civil conflict among the rival resistance groups posed excessive risk. Despite these failures, UNGOMAP may be considered an overall success because it gave assurance of Soviet good faith. U.S. interests were well served by having impartial monitors confirm the Soviet withdrawal.

The First United Nations Angola Verification Mission (UNAVEM I) successfully observed Cuban withdrawal from Angola. The United States and the Soviet Union induced their respective clients to cooperate. In addition, Cuba was willing to leave when the Luandan government declined to defray the cost of deployment. In any case, South Africa's withdrawal from Namibia eliminated the foreign threat to Angola. UNAVEM verified compliance and gave Cuba political cover for its withdrawal.

ONUCA was unable to detect violations of the 1987 Esquipulas II Agreements, although violations doubtless occurred. The operation was hampered by jungle vegetation and lack of night-vision devices for observing during darkness. The parties eventually fulfilled their agreements anyway, and ONUCA served a symbolic function by duly recording their compliance. In this operation, a technical failure made little difference because regional powers enthusiastically supported the peace process.

A state of civil war between the Angolan government and *União Nacional para a Independência Total de Angola* (UNITA), led by Jonas Savimbi, caused the Second United Nations Angola Verification Mission (UNAVEM II) to fail. The United States and Russia lost much of their interest in Angola after the end of the Cold War, leaving little motive to impel their former clients toward reconciliation.

The United Nations Preventive Deployment Force (UNPREDEP; formerly UNPROFOR) currently observes the borders of Macedonia with Albania and Yugoslavia (Serbia and Montenegro). Its underlying purpose is to underscore a U.S. diplomatic warning to Yugoslavia, an example of "preventive deployment" in U.N. terminology. If violations occurred, the Security Council would have to respond; otherwise, the operation would be exposed as a bluff. Belgrade earlier showed disinterest in Macedonia by withdrawing its forces, but it might be tempted to return if an Albanian uprising in Kosovo were supported by Albanians in Macedonia. Through late 1995, the most destabilizing foreign influence was a Greek embargo of Macedonia. To alleviate the effects of this embargo, the Security Council ignored Macedonia's trade with Serbia and Montenegro although that trade violated economic sanctions.

Interposition

Interposition succeeded because parties were willing to perpetuate the line of confrontation. But success tended to make interposition an interminable operation. Moreover, the presence of a peace-keeping force gave parties an excuse to procrastinate, avoiding ne-gotiations that might require them to abandon unattainable goals.[2] Figure 4.2 evaluates cases of interposition.

Interposition succeeded between Egyptian and Israeli forces after the 1956 war, although Israel refused to accept the presence of United Nations forces on its territory. UNEF I terminated when President Nasser requested that peace-keepers depart just prior to the Six Day War. After the Yom Kippur War in 1973, UNEF II was successful, de-

RANDMR582-4.2

Operation— Manpower	Mandate	Fulfilled?
UNEF I (Gaza, Sinai)— 6,073 in 1957	Form a buffer zone between Anglo-French and Egyptian forces; supervise withdrawal of Israeli forces from Sinai; patrol armistice lines.	Yes until 1967
UNEF II (Suez, Sinai)— 6,973 in 1974	Form a buffer zone between Egyptian and Israeli forces; supervise withdrawal of Israeli forces from Canal; inspect areas subject to arms limitations.	Yes
UNFICYP 1974–1994 (Cyprus)— 4,444 in 1974	Delineate the limit of Turkish advance; form a buffer zone between Turkish and Greek Cypriot forces; perform humanitarian functions.	Yes
UNDOF (Golan Heights)— 1,338 in 1990	Observe compliance with cease-fire; occupy area of separation between Israeli and Syrian forces; inspect forces in areas of limitation of armaments.	Yes
UNIKOM (Kuwait)— 1,440 in 1991	Deter violations of the Iraq-Kuwait border by monitoring activity in a demilitarized zone extending 10 km into Iraq and 5 km into Kuwait (preventive deployment).	Yes

Figure 4.2—Evaluating Interposition Operations

---

[2]"Often it is less difficult to keep a cease-fire in being than to resolve [the] original conflict. In such cases it is right for the Security Council to ask itself from time to time whether the peace-keeping operation has 'become part of the problem' by protecting the parties from the consequences of their negotiating stands. But it should not be as-sumed that longevity means that a peace-keeping operation has failed." United Nations, *Blue Helmets*, 1990, p. 8.

spite Israel's attempts to strangle the surrounded Egyptian Third Army. UNEF II not only helped Egypt and Israel to disengage their forces, it also helped the United States and Soviet Union to avoid confrontation on behalf of their respective allies. This operation was terminated when the Soviet Union refused to approve a mandate to help implement the April 25, 1979, peace treaty between Egypt and Israel.[3]

UNFICYP successfully interposed itself during the 1974 Turkish intervention on Cyprus and still remains in place. Interposition has helped the Greek-dominated Republic of Cyprus to remain the only internationally recognized government on the island. But at the same time, interposition has perpetuated the de facto partition of the island, an outcome satisfactory to Turkish Cypriots.

Beginning in 1974, U.N. forces have controlled a buffer zone between Israeli and Syrian forces on the Golan Heights, another successful operation with no end in sight. No foreseeable agreements between Israel and Syria are likely to obviate the need for international control over the Golan Heights. On the contrary, an Israeli-Syrian peace settlement will probably require long-term assurances that neither party is encroaching on this strategic territory.

Interposition on the Iraq-Kuwait border is a special case. It is intended to deter Iraqi aggression against Kuwait and depends on the power of the anti-Iraq coalition, especially that of the United States as its leading member. During October 1994, the United States and its allies increased their credibility by responding vigorously to threatening Iraqi deployments.

MORE-AMBITIOUS OPERATIONS

Transition

Transition operations usually succeeded at least partially, except in Croatia, where they failed. Success depended fundamentally on co-

---

[3]Instead, the peace treaty was facilitated by the newly created Multinational Force and Observers, built around an American infantry battalion. It absorbed the United States Sinai Field Mission, a small group of unarmed civilian observers maintaining a surveillance system.

operation from the parties and support from states that were not parties. Figure 4.3 evaluates transition operations.

UNTEA/UNSF oversaw a transition from Dutch colonial rule to Indonesian authority. It was successful because the United States mediated between Indonesia and the Netherlands, pressuring both sides to avoid war; the Dutch were willing to depart; Indonesia knew it could ensure a favorable plebiscite; and the August 15, 1962,

RAND*MR582-4.3*

Operation— Manpower	Mandate	Fulfilled?
UNTEA/UNSF (New Guinea)— 1,500 in 1962	Implement cease-fire; administer and secure western New Guinea; transfer administration to Indonesia; assist in plebiscite.	Yes
UNFICYP 1964–1974 (Cyprus)— 6,411 in 1964	Use best efforts to prevent recurrence of fighting; contribute to a return to normal conditions.	Partially
UNTAG (Namibia)— 4,493 in 1989	Monitor cease-fire and withdrawal of South African forces; monitor police activities; ensure free and fair elections to Constituent Assembly.	Yes
ONUCA (Nicaragua)— 1,098 in 1990	Monitor withdrawal of government forces; secure assembly areas; receive and destroy weapons of demobilized Contras.	Yes
MINURSO (Western Sahara)— 3,295 in 1992	Oversee cease-fire; monitor drawdown of Moroccan forces; register voters and conduct referendum on future of country.	Partially
ONUMOZ (Mozambique)— 7,000 in 1992	Monitor cease-fire; monitor separation of forces, demobilization, and disarmament; monitor electoral process; coordinate humanitarian assistance.	Yes
UNTAC (Cambodia)— 20,000 in 1993	Verify withdrawal of foreign forces; monitor cease-fire; implement demobilization through a cantonment system; secure free elections.	Partially
UNPROFOR[a] (Croatia)— 15,000 in 1994	Oversee demilitarization of United Nations Protected Areas in Croatia; see that persons are protected from armed attack.	No
UNAMIR (Rwanda)— 5,500 in 1994	Contribute to protection of displaced persons, refugees, and civilians at risk in Rwanda; secure and support distribution of relief supplies.	Partially

[a]Redesignated the United Nations Confidence Restoration Operation in Croatia (UNCRO) in 1995.

Figure 4.3—Evaluating Transition Operations

Dutch-Indonesian Accord exactly specified mandate and schedule for accomplishment of the transition.

UNFICYP could not restore normal conditions in Cyprus because the Turkish Cypriots refused to take part in a common government and because both sides continued to maintain militias. Until 1974, the United States successfully dissuaded the Turkish government from intervening in Cyprus but was unable to mediate a resolution. During the Greek coup in 1974, the United States failed to avert a Turkish intervention, which made the original UNFICYP mandate unworkable. The failure to accomplish the original mandate reflected on the parties, not on UNFICYP.

UNTAG succeeded for these reasons: The United States mediated among the parties and kept pressure on them; protracted negotiations gave ample time for preparation; South Africa was tired of the military stalemate and was willing to depart Namibia if the Cubans would leave Angola; Cuba was weary of its adventure in Angola; South Africa was allowed to defeat a SWAPO incursion that could have ruined the peace process; and a publicity campaign convinced Namibians to participate in the elections.

During early 1990, the United Nations Observer Group in Central America was augmented by a Venezuelan infantry battalion to conduct demobilization of the Contras in security zones established in Nicaragua. This demobilization was successful because the United States ceased to support the Contras following the advent of the Chamorro administration; the Central American governments were committed to the Esquipulas II Agreements; Honduras wanted the Contras to depart its territory; most Contras had confidence in the U.N.–monitored security zones; and the United States supported and financed the peace process. In this case, demobilization was wholly voluntary: ONUCA had no power or authority to compel the Contras to demobilize.

MINURSO monitored aspects of the cease-fire but could not ensure an impartial referendum on the future of the Western Sahara. Morocco obstructed freedom of movement and packed the voter registry with thousands of persons living outside the Western Sahara. Morocco felt confident of its military superiority and was determined to ensure a favorable outcome.

ONUMOZ was successful despite severe difficulties. After demobilization, the new national army was weak, and demobilized soldiers, who still possessed assault rifles and machine guns, disrupted public order. Although civil conflict now appears at an end, Mozambique remains in an unsettled state.

UNTAC verified withdrawal of Vietnamese forces from Cambodia, although it had difficulty distinguishing between troops and settlers of Vietnamese origin. UNTAC failed to implement demobilization because the Pol Pot faction of the Khmer Rouge refused to participate, causing the Vietnamese-installed government to also evade demobilization. (UNTAC successfully disarmed two smaller militias.) UNTAC devoted its efforts to securing free elections that resulted in a victory for the moderate Royalist party. The ultimate success of the peace process depends on the future of this government. UNTAC had neither the combat power nor the authority to fight any party in Cambodia, nor would the contributing member states have accepted such a mandate.

A transition operation failed in Croatia because the parties did not keep their agreements and because the peace force was entirely inadequate to maintain United Nations Protected Areas. UNPROFOR was too weak to protect any population, whether Croats subjected to "ethnic cleansing" or Croatian Serbs subjected to repeated attacks from Croatia. Partly because of these attacks, UNPROFOR also failed to disarm Serbs in the UNPAs. In March 1994, UNPROFOR assumed control over a buffer zone between Croatian and Croatian Serb forces along the line of confrontation. In August 1995, UNPROFOR, now called UNCRO, was swept aside when Croatian Army forces conducted a successful offensive into Krajina. In January 1996, the Security Council authorized a new transition operation in the last remaining Serb-held area of Croatia.[4]

UNAMIR was too weak to accomplish its transition mandate in Rwanda. Civil conflict began in Rwanda in 1959, when Hutus over-

---

[4]Recalling the failures of the past, Secretary General Boutros-Ghali recommended that transition of Eastern Slavonia from Serbian to Croatian authority, as agreed by the parties in November 1995 at Dayton, Ohio, should be implemented by over 9,000 troops controlled through some entity other than the U.N. He was overruled, and the Security Council authorized another U.N.–controlled operation (UNTAES) with an initial strength of 5,000 troops.

threw the Tutsi monarchy. After the Belgian protectorate ended in 1962, Tutsis tried unsuccessfully to topple the Hutu-dominated government, and many Tutsis fled to neighboring countries. In August 1993, the government and the Rwandan Patriotic Front (RPF) concluded the Arusha Peace Agreement, which foresaw a transitional government with representation from all parties. The following month, UNAMIR was established to help implement this agreement.

But on April 6, 1994, after the presidents of Rwanda and Burundi died in a suspicious plane crash, Hutu soldiers and militia went on a rampage, killing Tutsi civilians on a scale considered genocide by the Secretary-General. At the same time, the RPF invaded again from Uganda. UNAMIR then had 2,500 troops, too few to intervene effectively. After ten Belgian soldiers died trying to protect the moderate Hutu prime minister from Hutu death squads, Belgium withdrew its large contingent.

In May 1994, the Security Council gave UNAMIR a mandate to "contribute to the security and protection of displaced persons, refugees and civilians at risk in Rwanda"[5] with an authorized strength of 5,500 troops. But European states declined to participate, and African states that were willing to participate had to be provided heavy equipment, delaying their arrival. In late August, UNAMIR assumed responsibility for the area of southern Rwanda under French protection (Operation Turquoise). By this time, the RPF had extended its control over the entire country. Some 2 million Hutus had fled to neighboring countries, especially to Zaire, where they were controlled by elements of the former Hutu regime. Hutu leaders in exile prevented the refugees from returning and were apparently preparing to invade Rwanda.

In December 1995, the Security Council reduced UNAMIR to an authorized strength of 1,200 and gave it a mandate to exercise its good offices to promote voluntary repatriation of refugees and to assist the government of Rwanda in the safe return of refugees.[6] In January 1996, Canada, which had provided the Force Commander, an-

---

[5] Security Council Resolution 918 on May 17, 1994.
[6] Security Council Resolution 1029 on December 12, 1995.

nounced its decision to withdraw from UNAMIR on the grounds that its force structure was inadequate.[7]

Security for Humanitarian Aid

These operations have a mixed record of success and failure, depending primarily on the capabilities of the force. Even when they succeed, security operations are open to the criticism that they alleviate suffering without addressing the conflict that caused it. Therefore, suffering may recur for the same reasons after the peace force departs. Worse yet, humanitarian aid may even promote conflict by supplying combatants. For example, humanitarian aid to Hutu refugees in the Zaire camps might help them initiate a new episode of civil war in Rwanda. Aid to all parties in Bosnia-Herzegovina helped them to continue fighting despite their ruined economies. Figure 4.4 evaluates security operations.

RAND*MR582-4.4*

Operation— Manpower	Mandate	Fulfilled?
UNIFIL (Lebanon)— 5,904 in 1990	Confirm withdrawal of Israeli forces from Lebanon; restore peace and security in southern Lebanon; perform humanitarian functions.	Partially
UNOSOM I (Somalia)— 3,500 in 1992	Secure the delivery of humanitarian aid by protecting distribution centers and convoys.	No
UNITAF–UNOSOM (Somalia)— 28,000 in 1993	Provide security for humanitarian aid; suppress banditry and visible weapons; begin systematic disarmament of Somali factional militias (task added during operations).	Yes

Figure 4.4—Evaluating Security for Humanitarian Aid Operations

---

[7]"The decision to withdraw reflects the Canadian view that the mandate renewed in December 1995 is not viable, given the authorized force structure. . . .

This decision to withdraw from UNAMIR should not be construed as a lessening in any way of Canada's willingness to participate in the search for stability and security in the Great Lakes region of Africa or in our commitment to assist the Rwandan Government to rebuild its devastated country. It is, rather, a sign of our concern that the Security Council has not yet fully absorbed lessons learned from the recent past in peace-keeping operations." Letter, dated January 16, 1996, from the Permanent Representative of Canada to the United Nations, addressed to the Secretary-General, S/1996/35, January 17, 1996.

UNIFIL failed to fulfill an ambiguously worded transition mandate because southern Lebanon was fragmented among rival groups and heavily influenced by foreign powers. The situation became complicated because the Beirut government was unable to control southern Lebanon, leading Israel to invade and sponsor a friendly militia. Syria also invaded Lebanon and became heavily involved in Lebanese politics. In 1983, bombing of a Marine barracks caused the United States to withdraw its forces. Terrorist groups, including the Iran-supported Hezbollah, continued to operate throughout southern Lebanon. Unable to influence these events, UNIFIL made humanitarian aid its first priority.

UNOSOM I was established in April 1992 with 50 military observers and 500 troops—an inadequate force. Fighting among the factions and general lawlessness continued to impede delivery of aid and cause it to be diverted. In August, the Security Council authorized four 750-man security units to protect distribution points and truck convoys. Pakistan deployed an infantry battalion to Somalia during September, but the situation continued to deteriorate. At the same time, the United States began an airlift of humanitarian aid from neighboring Kenya.

In November, the Secretary-General found that UNOSOM I was unable to accomplish its mandate and accepted President Bush's offer to lead an operation (Restore Hope) that would ensure delivery of aid. UNOSOM I failed as a result of violent faction (clan) rivalries, efforts by faction leaders to control the delivery of aid for political purposes, the collapse of the central government, large quantities of weapons and ammunition left from the Barre regime, limited transportation infrastructure, and inadequate U.N. forces.

UNITAF successfully secured humanitarian aid because its large, highly capable forces overawed the rival clan leaders, coercing them to allow delivery. At the same time, UNITAF was authorized to use lethal force under Chapter VII, implying liberal rules of engagement. Under these rules, the U.S. 10th Mountain Division carried out a "Four No's" policy (No bandits, No checkpoints, No "technicals,"[8]

---

[8]To secure humanitarian aid, the United Nations had contracted for "technical assistance," a euphemism for security guards. The term "technicals" came to mean any light vehicle mounting a crew-served weapon.

No visible weapons). In addition, UNITAF initiated the collection of heavy weapons. These efforts at disarmament went well beyond security for humanitarian aid, but the United States resisted further mission creep, which might have delayed departure of U.S. forces (less the Quick Reaction Force that remained).

Peace Enforcement

Peace enforcement yielded extremely poor results. The only clear success occurred in the Congo, and even that victory was Pyrrhic for the United Nations. Operations in Somalia ended in failure, and operations in Bosnia-Herzegovina had very limited success. These poor results indicate that peace enforcement must be conducted differently if there is to be a reasonable prospect of success. Figure 4.5 evaluates peace enforcement operations.

Congo. *Operation des Nations Unies au Congo* failed to stabilize the Congo because the government divided between Lumumba and Kasavubu factions, the Congolese Army became hostile to ONUC, and tribal warfare spread throughout the country. At the same time, mineral-rich Katanga Province seceded with the support of European mining interests. After a false start, ONUC conducted combat operations to end that secession. In January 1963, an Indian infantry brigade supported by a Swedish fighter squadron regained Katanga

RAND*MR582-4.5*

Operation— Manpower	Mandate	Fulfilled?
ONUC (Congo)— 19,000 in 1961	Monitor withdrawal of Belgian forces; stabilize the Congo through presence; capture and expel mercenaries; end secession of Katanga Province (actual purpose of operations by Indian brigade).	Partially
UNOSOM II–U.S. (Somalia)— 20,000 in 1993	Secure humanitarian aid; collect weapons in accordance with the Addis Ababa agreements; arrest those responsible for armed attacks on UNOSOM II.	No
UNPROFOR–NATO (Bosnia)— 24,000 in 1995[a]	Secure humanitarian aid; open Sarajevo airport; enforce no-fly zone; see that safe areas are free from armed attack; enforce exclusion zones associated with safe areas.	Partially

[a]Includes 6,000 troops in Rapid Reaction Force.

Figure 4.5—Evaluating Peace Enforcement Operations

Province and expelled the mercenary forces (Operation Grandslam). But when ONUC ceased operations in June 1964, the Congo was wracked by civil conflict, which ended when Joseph-Désiré Mobutu assumed power.

The Congo operation was highly controversial, causing a constitutional and financial crisis in the U.N. The crisis occurred because France and the Soviet Union, plus its satellites, refused to pay assessments for ONUC, eventually totaling more than two years' regular assessments. According to Article 19 of the Charter, France and the Soviet Union should have lost their voting rights in the General Assembly. Rather than pursue this issue, perhaps at the cost of disrupting the U.N., the United States funded over half the costs itself and promoted a bond issue. This crisis inhibited peace operations for at least a decade. Still, ONUC advanced American interests by preventing great-power conflict in Africa at the height of the Cold War.

Somalia. UNOSOM II, plus an American light infantry battalion controlled through national channels, attempted to facilitate a national reconciliation of rival factions as agreed in Addis Ababa, including disarmament. But after Mohammed Farah Aideed evaded disarmament and eventually attacked the Pakistani contingent, the Security Council resolved that those responsible for the attack be brought to justice. American special-operations forces attempted to capture Aideed and his principal supporters, primarily through heliborne raids in Mogadishu. On October 3, 1993, the United States lost 18 men as the result of such a raid. Four days later, President Clinton announced that the United States would withdraw its forces from Somalia by March 1994. UNOSOM II waited vainly for the faction leaders to resolve their differences, until being extracted with U.S. assistance in March 1995.

UNOSOM II failed because it was not properly related to the preceding UNITAF and because it depended on U.S. participation, which proved half-hearted. The operations were improperly related in that a powerful, U.S.–controlled UNITAF left the dangerous task of disarmament to a weak, U.N.–controlled UNOSOM II. Either UNITAF should have disarmed the factions or the Security Council should have given UNOSOM II a less ambitious mandate. Saddled with a mandate that exceeded its grasp, UNOSOM II was critically dependent on the United States. Lacking interest in Somalia, the United States deployed only small, light forces, which were compelled to operate at considerable risk. When the almost-inevitable casualties occurred, the United States immediately abandoned peace enforcement and soon withdrew altogether, leaving UNOSOM II without a workable mandate.

Bosnia-Herzegovina. The Security Council repeatedly invoked Chapter VII for operations in Bosnia, but member states did not provide sufficiently powerful ground forces. In addition, the United Nations Protection Force remained under U.N. control, an arrangement unsuitable for combat operations. During 1993, the Council accepted offers of NATO air support to enforce no-fly zones, to provide close air support to UNPROFOR, and to protect the populations of safe areas. But UNPROFOR persistently refused to request or approve air strikes, fearing retaliation from the Bosnian Serbs.

UNPROFOR and NATO compiled a mixed record in securing humanitarian aid. UNPROFOR secured the Sarajevo airport even though the parties did not fulfill their agreements to withdraw weapons from the vicinity of Sarajevo airport and not to impede flight operations. For several years, Sarajevo was sustained primarily through airlift. UNPROFOR failed to secure truck convoys transporting humanitarian aid through Serb-held territory. Humanitarian agencies distributed much aid to Croats and Serbs, whether needed or not, as the price for reaching Muslims. Even so, Bosnian Serbs blocked aid to Muslim enclaves for months at a time in an effort to starve the populations into submission. The United States and other powers avoided this land blockade by airdropping supplies.

UNPROFOR and NATO generally failed to keep the populations of the six safe areas free from armed attack. Moreover, Bosnian Serbs continued to bombard and to attack several safe areas, including Sarajevo. After 68 civilians were killed by a single explosion in Sarajevo on February 5, 1994, NATO issued an ultimatum declaring an exclusion zone around the city. It threatened to attack heavy weapons within this exclusion zone, except those placed in collection points operated by UNPROFOR. The parties complied with this ultimatum. However, a few weeks later, Bosnian Serbs attacked the Gorazde safe area, and in the fall they attacked the Bihac safe area.

In both instances the Serbs claimed to be responding to attacks from the Muslim side.

During early 1995, heavy fighting occurred around Sarajevo and Bosnian Serbs recovered some heavy weapons from the collection points. In late May, the UNPROFOR commander issued an ultimatum to cease firing heavy weapons within the exclusion zone. After Bosnian Serbs ignored this ultimatum, NATO attacked military targets near Pale, the Bosnian Serb capital. In response, Bosnian Serbs took several hundred UNPROFOR personnel hostage, handcuffing some to military facilities to avert NATO air attack.

This crisis provoked public disagreements among the United States and its European allies. With no forces on the ground, the United States advocated stronger measures; Britain and France, whose ground forces were at risk, showed reluctance and debated whether to reinforce or terminate operations. Republican leaders in Congress announced that they would approve reinforcement on condition that the United States neither pay for it nor contribute forces. Britain, France, and the Netherlands decided to deploy a Rapid Reaction Force capable of responding to exigencies.[9]

On July 6, 1995, Bosnian Serb forces began attacking the safe area of Srebrenica held by a Dutch mechanized infantry battalion. By the end of the day, the Serbs overran several observation posts, taking several Dutch soldiers hostage and looting their weapons and equipment, including several light armored vehicles. After repeated requests from the Dutch battalion commander, the UNPROFOR Force Commander in Zagreb decided around noon on July 10 to authorize close air support. Two hours later, NATO aircraft attacked two Serb tanks.

In response, the Bosnian Serb General Ratko Mladic announced that he would kill the 30 Dutch soldiers held by Serbs and destroy Srebrenica unless NATO stopped air attacks. The Dutch Minister of Defense demanded that air attacks be stopped. The following day,

---

[9]The Rapid Reaction Force was originally planned to comprise three brigades, including one held in reserve in France. Elements of this force deployed to south-central Bosnia, where they kept the Mount Igman road open and eventually provided counterbattery fire to help lift the siege of Sarajevo.

Bosnian Serb forces seized the Srebrenica safe area, compelling some 30,000 Muslims to flee. Approximately 12,000 able-bodied Muslim men attempted to trek 60 miles overland to Muslim-held territory. Thousands of these men were captured by Bosnian Serbs and massacred. A week later, Serb forces seized the Zepa safe area, leaving Gorazde the last Muslim-held enclave in eastern Bosnia.

On August 28, 1995, a shell killed 37 people in the same open-air market where 68 had been killed in February of the previous year, prompting the first NATO ultimatum. This time, NATO conducted a two-week bombing offensive against Bosnian Serbs. The Serbs were unable to seize hostages because UNPROFOR had withdrawn from exposed positions, including the Gorazde safe area. On September 14, the Bosnian Serb leaders agreed to all demands, including unobstructed land traffic into Sarajevo. What effect the NATO air offensive had is not entirely certain, because during August and September the Serbs were also subjected to successful Croat and Muslim ground offensives that cost them Krajina and about 20 percent of Bosnia-Herzegovina. This change in the military balance, coupled with U.S. leadership and Serbian pressure on the Bosnian Serbs, led to the Dayton Agreements.

Bosnia-Herzegovina demonstrated that peace operations with consent and peace enforcement are incompatible and should not be mingled: either the deployed force has consent and expects immunity or it operates without consent and accepts the risks of combat. It should not attempt to operate in a shadowland between these starkly different alternatives.

Bosnia-Herzegovina also revealed a propensity in the Security Council to adopt strongly worded resolutions that member states were not prepared to enforce, causing an erosion of credibility. The fall of the Srebrenica safe area is the most discrediting episode in the history of U.N. peace operations.

SUMMARY

The Security Council has often succeeded in traditional peacekeeping and has had some success in more-ambitious peace operations under Chapter VI. But the Council has failed repeatedly, sometimes catastrophically, when it has attempted operations under

Chapter VII, even when great powers participated. Failure in coercive peace operations is rooted in the more fundamental failure of collective security under the Charter of the United Nations.

Peace-Keeping

Traditional peace-keeping has helped parties to implement their agreements. It has tended to succeed when the agreements were viable, i.e., were concluded bona fide because the parties believed that the agreements were compatible with their interests and were preferable to continuing a violent conflict.

But why should the Security Council be expected to help parties implement agreements that are in their own interests? There are several, often interrelated, reasons:

- The parties may be so swayed by mutual animosity and suspicion that they need an impartial intermediary.

- Each party may hesitate to fulfill agreements unless it is reliably informed that other parties are also in compliance.

- The parties may be willing to disengage their forces, yet may be fearful that their adversaries will renege and gain advantages.

A peace-keeping force can allay these fears by controlling buffer zones that include strategically important terrain. In addition, peace-keeping can affect states that are not parties, yet are interested in the outcome. For example, the great powers have used peace-keeping to help limit and contain their own rivalry, especially in the Middle East.

More-Ambitious Operations

More-ambitious operations typically have involved demobilization and new governmental structures, which have often provoked opposition from parties that felt their power was threatened.

Under Chapter VI. Noncoercive transition operations have tended to succeed once the parties exhausted their hope of obtaining better results through violence and once other states gave active support to the peace process, keeping the parties under pressure to maintain their agreements. Operations in Namibia, Nicaragua, and Mozambique have fit this pattern.

As might be anticipated, some parties reneged on their agreements when their power appeared threatened. Examples include the Pol Pot faction of the Khmer Rouge in Cambodia, *União Nacional para a Independência Total de Angola* (UNITA) in Angola, and Serbs in Croatia. In those operations, the Security Council deplored breaches of agreements but did not attempt to enforce compliance. It allowed parts of the original mandate to fall into abeyance (Cambodia), terminated the peace operation (Angola), or accepted a lesser mandate before the operation was swept away (Croatia). While such behavior may appear ignoble for an organization with the authority of the Security Council, it is surely preferable to half-hearted attempts at enforcement.

Under Chapter VII. By invoking Chapter VII, the Security Council has indicated a willingness to apply force, if necessary, to coerce parties that defy its resolutions. The Council has therefore assumed the role of a potential combatant, compelling the parties to assess the probable consequences if they oppose the Council. Parties were unlikely to defy the Council if they believed it had the political will and the military force to coerce them successfully. Such deterrence occurred when the United States deployed powerful forces under its own control (Multinational Force in Haiti, Unified Task Force in Somalia). Although international in a formal sense, those operations were fundamentally U.S. initiatives conducted under authority of the Security Council.

Absent strong U.S. participation, the Security Council has neither demonstrated the political will nor assembled the military force needed to coerce parties. Perceiving this weakness, parties have ignored resolutions under Chapter VII and have openly defied the Council. Examples include Mohammed Farah Aideed's faction in Mogadishu and the Bosnian Serb authorities in Pale. In those instances, the Council made half-hearted attempts at peace enforcement and suffered ignominious failures.

Peace enforcement has failed for the same reason that collective security has failed: lack of a sufficiently strong consensus for action among permanent members of the Security Council. Moreover, peace enforcement has special complications and difficulties. Complications ensue because more than one party can be recalcitrant, either successively or simultaneously. For example, Bosnian Muslims and Bosnian Serbs both violated provisions concerning safe areas, although the Serb violations were more egregious. Difficulties arise because impartiality demands that the Security Council forgo the benefits of having allies among parties to the conflict. In the same example, it was precluded from arming and training Bosnian Muslim forces to resist attacks on safe areas.

Chapter Five

CONCLUSIONS

An operational perspective, as adopted in this report, generates a useful typology of peace operations. Such a typology promotes a differentiated view that avoids blanket praise or condemnation of such operations. It allows fruitful comparisons among operations of similar type. Finally, it provides a basis for reforming peace operations.

A DIFFERENTIATED VIEW

It is tempting to idealize peace operations at one extreme or to denigrate them at the other extreme. Those who believe that a responsible international community exists or can be created are inclined to romanticize peace operations. To a sympathetic observer, the mere appearance of a peace operation is immensely appealing. Contingents from many states join forces—not to fight a war for national interests but to promote peace for the common good. They fly the flag of an organization committed in principle to the highest ideals of humanity, as the United States is committed.

But those who believe that a responsible international community is fantasy or an undesirable trammel are inclined to denigrate peace operations. Undeniably, peace operations are poorly organized and are often badly equipped when compared with the military operations of great powers. To an unsympathetic eye, they seem an excuse to remunerate impecunious states: at best a make-work project and at worst a pious hoax.

There is little point in undifferentiated praise or condemnation. Peace operations will not bring in the millennium, but they can make valuable contributions to peace. Their contributions should be understood in the context of an operational typology. Some types of operations, especially those associated with traditional peace-keeping, have been competently performed through the U.N. system and have been well worth the expense. Other types of operations, especially those under Chapter VII that went to peace enforcement, have demanded more commitment from great powers than those powers were willing to make and have brought costly failures. The primary cause of these failures was lack of determination among the great powers, not some failing of the admittedly imperfect U.N. or some inherent flaw in peace operations.

FRUITFUL COMPARISONS

The typology presented in this report allows fruitful comparisons among peace operations of the same type. It is fruitful, for example, to review the records of observer forces to discern what activities are accessible to observation, what reconnaissance means are required, and how much cooperation is needed from the parties. Comparisons are also helpful when they reveal prerequisites for success and root causes of failure: Why did interposition succeed in the Near East and again in Cyprus, but fail catastrophically in Croatia? What factors account for this dramatic difference that could help the Security Council recognize when interposition is likely to fail? Particularly instructive are comparisons among transition operations, a type that has burgeoned in the past few years, involves complex mandates, and demands close coordination with numerous civilian organizations.

Comparing operations of the same type can support efforts to develop rapid response within the U.N. system. It appears unlikely that the Security Council will ever command large-scale forces commensurate with its responsibilities under Chapter VII. But the Council may well have small-scale forces at its disposal that are ready to conduct the repertoire of traditional peace-keeping under Chapter VI. Comparison of past operations should allow planners to discern accurately what organization, equipment, and training would be appropriate for such forces undertaking a particular type of operation.

BASIS FOR REFORM

Peace operations must be reformed; otherwise, their future will be very bleak. By early 1996, the Security Council was suffering a severe loss of reputation through humiliating failures in places such as Mogadishu and Srebrenica. At the same time, the U.N. system was plunged into financial crisis by refusal of member states, especially the United States, to pay their assessments. These two developments were related: Congressional reluctance to pay for peace operations was deepened by failures, especially what was seen as betrayal of the Bosnian Muslims.

The most urgent reform is for the Security Council to see peace operations from an operational perspective rather than from a more political perspective. In recent years, the Council has passed far more resolutions than previously, including many that the parties ignored. Being ignored is problematic because it diminishes the prestige of the Security Council. But the Council has done far greater harm by giving unrealistic mandates to Force Commanders. An operational perspective on peace operations should help decisionmakers to frame mandates that are appropriate to the situation and to the capabilities of the peace force.

TERMS USED IN THIS REPORT

This appendix provides definitions for terms used in the report.

Chapter VI: (1) Articles 33 through 38 of the Charter of the United Nations, concerning the pacific settlement of disputes; (2) authority conferred by the Security Council to employ lethal force in self-defense while accomplishing a mandate.

Chapter VII: (1) Articles 39 through 51 of the Charter of the United Nations, concerning action with respect to threats to the peace, breaches of the peace, and acts of aggression; (2) authority conferred by the Security Council to employ lethal force beyond self-defense to accomplish a mandate.

Combined: Inclusion of more than one state, e.g., the United States, France, and Britain. (American military usage)

Command: "Authority over subordinates by virtue of rank or assignment to accomplish assigned missions." (Joint Chiefs of Staff, 1986, p. 3-1) "No President has ever relinquished command over U.S. forces. Command constitutes the authority to issue orders covering every aspect of military operations and administration. The sole source of legitimacy for U.S. commanders originates from the U.S. Constitution, federal law and the Uniform Code of Military Justice and flows from the President to the lowest U.S. commander in the field.[1] The chain of command from the President to the lowest

---

[1] The qualifying phrase "in the field" is puzzling. Command is exerted in garrison and during a movement, as well as in the field. In the United States Army, the lowest echelon of command is company, battery, troop, or separate detachment.

commander in the field remains inviolate."[2]   (U.S. Department of State, 1994, p. 10.)

Conflict: Deliberate, organized use of lethal force, at a level exceeding terrorism, to attain political aims.

Consent: The evident willingness of parties, so far as they exist, to help accomplish a mandate. In the absence of parties, consent might be given by a legitimate government. Formal consent is manifested in statements, declarations, accords, agreements, etc. Actual consent is apparent from the behavior of the parties in the course of a peace operation. *Consent* is a complex phenomenon affected by the parties' aims, the balance of power, influence of other powers, and the effectiveness of peace operations, among other factors.

Diplomacy: (1) Conduct of relations among sovereign states by their heads or accredited representatives, (2) activities listed under Chapter VI, Article 33 of the Charter of the United Nations: negotiation, inquiry, mediation, conciliation, arbitration, judicial settlement, resort to regional agencies or arrangements, and other peaceful means.

Enforcement: A force acting under authority of the Security Council is expected to restore international peace and security by combat operations against a uniquely identified aggressor. There is no requirement for impartiality or consent; therefore, enforcement falls outside the definition of *peace operations*.

Great power: State with influence beyond its region through some combination of wealth, military power, and traditional leadership.

Impartiality: Refusal to take sides in a conflict, based on the judgment that the parties share responsibility. In the context of a peace operation, impartiality implies that the Security Council does not intend to attain the aims of one party, or group of parties, to the exclusion of others' aims. *It does not imply that every action taken by the*

---

[2]Not only the United States but virtually all sovereign states maintain an inviolate chain of command. Note that the term *command* is often used loosely. For example, the U.N. traditionally uses the term *Force Commander*, but this officer does not command forces (except his own national contingent); he only controls them. Indeed, a Force Commander usually has weak control over forces, much weaker than operational control in U.S. practice.

Security Council or states acting on its behalf will be neutral, i.e., will affect all parties equally or in the same way.[3]

Joint: Inclusion of two or more services, e.g., U.S. Army and U.S. Marine Corps. (American military usage)

Mandate: Formal expression of the purpose and scope of an operation. A mandate may be expressed through Security Council resolutions, peace plans, agreements among parties, and mission statements by powers acting under authority of the Security Council.

Non-governmental organization: An organization that is independent of state authority and recognized by the Economic and Social Council of the United Nations as having experience or technical knowledge of value to the Council's work. (United Nations usage)

Operational control: "Authority to perform those functions of command over subordinate forces involving organizing and employing commands and forces, assigning tasks, designating objectives, and giving authoritative direction necessary to accomplish the mission." (Joint Chiefs of Staff, 1986, p. 3-15) "Operational control is a subset of command. It is given for a specific time frame or mission and includes the authority to assign tasks to U.S. forces already deployed by the President, and assign tasks to U.S. troops led by U.S. officers. Within the limits of operational control, a foreign UN commander *cannot:* change the mission or deploy U.S. forces outside the area of responsibility agreed to by the President,[4] separate units, divide their supplies, administer discipline, promote anyone, or change their internal organization." (U.S. Department of State, 1994, p. 10)

---

[3]It is unlikely that any action, even just observing and reporting on behavior, could affect all parties equally or in the same way. The Security Council remains impartial, even when it enforces its will against a recalcitrant party, so long as this peace enforcement is intended to facilitate a resolution accommodating all parties. Parties do not have this Olympian perspective and usually perceive the Security Council as acting in a partisan fashion, i.e., in a manner that favors their opponents.

[4]An *area of responsibility* might be some part of the entire area encompassed by the mandate. If so, disallowing the authority to order deployment outside the area of responsibility can be a significant limitation on the Force Commander. For example, the UNOSOM commander could not order national contingents to deploy outside their assigned regions in Somalia without approval from home governments.

Party: An entity held to share responsibility for a conflict, e.g., the self-declared "Republic of Serbian Krajina" in 1991. Historically, the Security Council has recognized as "parties" rival clan leaders, representatives of ethnic communities, commanders of military formations, self-declared governments, and sovereign states.

Peace enforcement: A type of peace operation in which the peace force is expected to coerce recalcitrant parties into complying with their agreements or with resolutions of the Security Council.

Peace force: Military component of a peace operation. This force may range from unarmed observers to a joint and combined task force capable of sustained, large-scale combat.

Peace-keeping: (1) "Deployment of a United Nations presence in the field, hitherto with the consent of all the parties concerned, normally involving United Nations military and/or police personnel, and frequently civilians as well. Peace-keeping is a technique that expands the possibilities for both the prevention of conflict and the making of peace." (Boutros-Ghali, 1995) (2) "As the United Nations practice has evolved over the years, a peace-keeping operation has come to be defined as an operation involving military personnel, but without enforcement powers, undertaken by the United Nations to help maintain or restore international peace and security in areas of conflict. These operations are voluntary and are based on consent and co-operation. While they involve the use of military personnel, they achieve their objectives not by force of arms, thus contrasting them with the 'enforcement action' of the United Nations under Article 42. Peace-keeping operations have been most commonly employed to supervise and help maintain cease-fires, to assist in troop withdrawals, and to provide a buffer between opposing forces." (United Nations, *Blue Helmets*, 1990, pp. 4–5) (3) Observation or interposition with consent of the parties. (This study; derived from cases)

Peace operation: Use of force to allay conflict based on initial consent of the parties and impartiality toward them. However, parties may vanish, leaving a sole legitimate government as the source of consent, e.g, western New Guinea, Haiti.

Permanent Five: The five powers listed in Article 23 of the Charter of the United Nations, i.e., Republic of China, France, Union of Soviet

Socialist Republics (Russia), United Kingdom of Great Britain and Northern Ireland, and the United States of America. These are the prominent members of the winning coalition of World War II.

Regional power: State below great-power status having inherent ability to affect the outcome of a nearby conflict.

Rules of engagement: Directives concerning the use of lethal force, normally promulgated by the senior commander in an area of operations. Rules of engagement implement the general guidance implied by a mandate, including the invocation of Chapter VI or Chapter VII.

AGENDA FOR PEACE

This appendix provides a précis and brief analysis of a typology provided by the Secretary-General of the United Nations. The Secretary-General characterizes peace operations as, among other things, keeping, making, building, or enforcing peace.

PRÉCIS

In June 1992, Secretary-General Boutros Boutros-Ghali provided to the Security Council an "analysis and recommendations on ways of strengthening and making more efficient within the framework and provisions of the Charter the capacity of the United Nations for preventive diplomacy, for peacemaking and for peace-keeping."[1] In this report, he defines peace operations as follows:

"Preventive diplomacy is action to prevent disputes from arising between parties, to prevent existing disputes from escalating into conflicts and to limit the spread of the latter when they occur."[2] As examples, the Secretary-General outlines measures for confidence-building, fact-finding, early warning, preventive deployment, and establishment of demilitarized zones.[3] He broadly defines *preventive deployment* as deploying U.N. forces along international borders or

---

[1]United Nations, *Preventive Diplomacy, Peacemaking and Peace-Keeping: Report of the Secretary-General Pursuant to the Statement Adopted by the Summit Meeting of the Security Council on 31 January 1992,* A/47/277, S/24111, New York, June 17, 1992; hereafter *Agenda for Peace—1992.*

[2]United Nations, *Agenda for Peace—1992,* 1992, Paragraph 20.

[3]United Nations, *Agenda for Peace—1992,* 1992, Paragraph 23.

within a country in crisis. "In conditions of crisis within a country, when the Government requests or all parties consent, preventive deployment could help in a number of ways to alleviate suffering and to limit or control violence."[4]

"*Peacemaking* is action to bring hostile parties to agreement, essentially through peaceful means as those foreseen in Chapter VI of the Charter of the United Nations."[5] The expression "essentially through peaceful means" implies that the Security Council might use warlike means to make peace. After reviewing peaceful means under Chapter VI, Boutros-Ghali reviews the possibility of coercive measures under Chapter VII. He observes that "the Security Council has not so far made use of the most coercive of these measures—the action by military force foreseen in Article 42."[6] Indeed, he believes that forces available to the U.N. "may perhaps never be large or well enough equipped to deal with a threat from a major army equipped with sophisticated weapons."[7] But he recommends that the Security Council consider using "*peace enforcement units*" that would be on call and more heavily armed than peace-keeping forces. He foresees that "peace enforcement units" might be used to "restore and maintain the cease-fire."[8]

"*Peace-keeping* is the deployment of a United Nations presence in the field, hitherto with the consent[9] of all the parties concerned, normally involving United Nations military and/or police personnel

---

[4]United Nations, *Agenda for Peace—1992*, 1992, Paragraph 29. The phrase "all parties consent" implies that the Secretary-General envisions factions competing for control over a country. The words *suffering* and *violence* suggest that the crisis must be verging on conflict. Such circumstances make the expression "*preventive* deployment" seem oddly chosen, but the Secretary-General evidently means that the peace force could prevent the conflict from worsening or spreading.

[5]United Nations, *Agenda for Peace—1992*, 1992, Paragraph 20.

[6]United Nations, *Agenda for Peace—1992*, 1992, Paragraph 42. This statement covers all cases, including Korea and Kuwait, because these enforcement actions were carried out by member states acting *under authority of* the U.N., not *by* the U.N.

[7]United Nations, *Agenda for Peace—1992*, 1992, Paragraph 43.

[8]United Nations, *Agenda for Peace—1992*, 1992, Paragraph 44.

[9]The expression "hitherto with consent" muddies the definition because it implies that the Security Council might undertake "peace-keeping" without consent. But if it were undertaken without consent during an ongoing conflict, what would distinguish "peace-keeping" from "peace enforcement"?

and frequently civilians as well. Peace-keeping is a technique that expands the possibilities for both the prevention of conflict and the making of peace."[10] Boutros-Ghali considers "peace-keeping" an invention of the U.N. that has evolved rapidly in recent years and may not have precise boundaries: "Just as diplomacy will continue across the span of all the activities dealt with in the present report, so there may not be a dividing line between peacemaking and peace-keeping."[11]

"... *peace-building*—action to identify and support structures which will tend to strengthen and solidify peace in order to avoid a relapse into conflict."[12]

ANALYSIS

Figure B.1 presents a schematic overview of the typology contained in *Agenda for Peace—1992*.

The typology contained in *Agenda for Peace* is difficult to apply because it defines operations by progress toward "peace," an ambiguously defined concept. Does "peace" imply absence of armed conflict among states or other parties? Or does it imply an acceptable degree of civil order? In a recent example, Krajina Serbs conducted "ethnic cleansing" while fitfully observing a fragile cease-fire. Was there "peace" or not? Would "peace" imply fewer cease-fire violations, or fewer persons driven from their homes, or some mixture of both?

However "peace" were defined, it would be infinitely variable and subject to sudden changes, making a typology based on "peace" of doubtful practicality. Even among states, "peace" is highly variable. To what extent are Israel and Syria, or India and Pakistan, currently at "peace"?

Variability becomes much greater for protracted conflict between factions within a state, such as Somalia during 1992–1995. During

---

[10]United Nations, *Agenda for Peace—1992*, 1992, Paragraph 20.

[11]United Nations, *Agenda for Peace—1992*, 1992, Paragraph 45.

[12]United Nations, *Agenda for Peace—1992*, 1992, Paragraph 21.

RAND*MR582-B.1*

	Preventive Deployment	Peace-Keeping[a]	Peacemaking[a]		Peace-Building
			Peacemaking (peaceful means)	Peace Enforcement	
Chapter of the U.N. Charter	Chapter VI	Chapter VI (also Chapter VII?)	Chapter VI	Article 40, Chapter VII	Chapter VI
Consent Required from the Parties	Request of Government or all parties or with their consent (Paragraph 28)	"Hitherto with consent" (Paragraph 20) Cooperate in implementing mandate (Paragraph 50)	"Seek a solution" to differences (Paragraph 34)		Cooperate in "construction of a new environment" (Paragraph 57)
Typical Mandate	Deploy on both sides or one side of border; provide humanitarian aid; maintain security (Paragraphs 28, 29)	Provide presence to prevent conflict or to make peace (Paragraph 20)	Bring hostile parties to agreement essentially through peaceful means (Paragraph 20)	"Respond to outright aggression, imminent or actual" (Paragraph 44)	Disarm parties; restore order; repatriate refugees; train security personnel; monitor elections; protect human rights; reform governmental institutions (Paragraph 55)

[a] "... there may not be a dividing line between peacemaking and peace-keeping. Peacemaking is often a prelude to peace-keeping." (United Nations, *Agenda for Peace—1992*, 1992, Paragraph 45)

Figure B.1—Typology of Peace Operations in *Agenda for Peace—1992*

those years, much of Somalia was peaceful, although parts of the country were plagued by violent power struggles and sheer banditry. During roughly the same period, Bosnia-Herzegovina presented an even more complicated picture of civil conflict overlaid with conflict among states, interrupted by numerous cease-fires, and influenced by informal local agreements. A typology of peace operations that depends on the condition of "peace" would imply bewildering shifts among peace-keeping, peacemaking, and peace-building as the condition of "peace" changed.

Compounding these difficulties, *Agenda for Peace—1992* allows types of operations to overlap in a confusing way. "Peace-keeping" is not clearly differentiated from "peacemaking" nor given any definite content. "Peace-making" includes radically dissimilar operations, ranging from traditional peace-keeping through peace enforcement under Chapter VII. This exceptionally wide definition is confusing and unhelpful.

Buried within *Agenda for Peace—1992* is an urgent warning to the Security Council concerning the safety of U.N. personnel:

> Given the pressing need to afford adequate protection to United Nations personnel engaged in life-endangering circumstances, I recommend that the Security Council, unless it elects immediately to withdraw the United Nations personnel in order to preserve the credibility of the Organization, gravely consider what action should be taken towards those who put United Nations personnel in danger.[13]

Boutros-Ghali suggests that, before deployment occurs, the Council should consider what actions it will take, including those under Chapter VII, if parties frustrate the operation and hostilities occur. Subsequent events in Somalia and Bosnia-Herzegovina gave this warning a prophetic ring.

In January 1995, Boutros-Ghali revisited *Agenda for Peace—1992*. In addition to the typology offered previously, he identified a "new type of United Nations operation":

> This [reference to humanitarian aid] has led in Bosnia and Herzegovina and in Somalia to a new type of United Nations operation. Even though the use of force is authorized under Chapter VII of the Charter, the United Nations remains neutral and impartial between the warring parties, without a mandate to stop the aggressor (if one can be identified)[14] or impose a cessation of hostilities. Nor is this peace-keeping as practiced hitherto, because the hostilities continue and there is often no agreement between the warring parties on which a peace mandate can be based. The "safe areas" concept in Bosnia and Herzegovina is a similar case.[15]

---

[13]United Nations, *Agenda for Peace—1992*, 1992, Paragraph 67.

[14]This formulation confuses an important issue. Of course, the Council might identify an aggressor, deplore its aggression, and decline to take action. But would it be politically feasible or morally defensible for the Council to identify an aggressor and take actions designed to preserve impartiality between it and its victims? Almost certainly not, and therefore Boutros-Ghali should have offered a clear dichotomy: either the Council has decided to be impartial among warring parties or it has identified an aggressor and therefore is not impartial.

[15]United Nations, *Supplement to An Agenda for Peace: Position Paper of the Secretary-General on the Occasion of the Fiftieth Anniversary of the United Nations*, A/50/60, S/1995/1, New York, January 3, 1995, Paragraph 19; hereafter, *Agenda for Peace—1995*.

The statement that the U.N. "remains neutral and impartial" raises difficulties. Was it neutral to authorize the arrest of Mohammed Farah Aideed in Somalia? To defend Muslim-populated safe areas against Serb attacks using NATO air power? These actions were *impartial* in that they were not intended to attain the overall political goals of any party to the conflict, but they were certainly not *neutral*, in the sense of affecting all parties equally. On the contrary, they were largely or exclusively directed against certain parties considered obstructive to the peace process.

Boutros-Ghali assessed the causes of failure in Somalia and Bosnia-Herzegovina as follows:

> In reality, nothing is more dangerous for a peace-keeping operation than to ask it to use force when its existing composition, armament, logistic support and deployment deny it the capability to do so. The logic of peace-keeping flows from political and military premises that are quite distinct from those of enforcement; and the dynamics of the latter are incompatible with the political process that peace-keeping is intended to facilitate. To blur the distinction between the two can undermine the viability of the peace-keeping operation and endanger its personnel.[16]

The Secretary-General correctly argued that failure had two causes: (1) changing to peace enforcement mandates without providing the required forces and (2) attempting to combine incompatible types of operations, i.e., traditional peace-keeping and peace enforcement. He might have added that viable agreements among the parties are prerequisites for all peace operations based on continuous consent. In the absence of viable agreements, peace-keeping is ineffective and dangerous to the peace force—especially in Bosnia-Herzegovina. There, the Security Council mounted traditional peace-keeping operations to implement agreements that were ephemeral and usually *male fide*; therefore, those operations were ill-conceived and were failing even before the Security Council made half-hearted attempts at peace enforcement.

---

[16]United Nations, *Agenda for Peace—1995,* 1995, Paragraph 35.

Albright, Madeleine, "The Myths About U.N. Peacekeeping," *Statement to the House Foreign Affairs Subcommittee on International Security, International Organizations, and Human Rights,* Washington, D.C., June 24, 1993.

Allard, Kenneth, *Somalia Operations: Lessons Learned,* National Defense University Press, Washington, D.C., 1995.

Allen, William W., Antione D. Johnson, and John T. Nelsen II, "Peacekeeping and Peace Enforcement Operations," *Military Review,* October 1993, pp. 53–61.

Armstrong, Charles L., "From Futility to Insanity: A Brief Review of U.N. Failures," *Military Technology,* December 1994, pp. 89–91.

Baehr, Peter R., and Leon Gordenker, *The United Nations in the 1990s,* St. Martin's Press, New York, 1992.

Berkowitz, Bruce D., "Rules of Engagement for U.N. Peacekeeping Forces in Bosnia," *Orbis,* Fall 1994, pp. 635–646.

Betts, Richard K., "The Delusion of Impartial Intervention," *Foreign Affairs,* November/December 1994, pp. 20–33.

Blechman, Barry M., and J. Matthew Vaccaro, *Training for Peacekeeping: The United Nations' Role,* The Henry L. Stimson Center, Washington, D.C., Report No. 12, July 1994.

Boutros-Ghali, Boutros, *An Agenda for Peace—1995* (presenting United Nations, *Supplement to Agenda for Peace,* A/50/60-

S/1995/1), Department of Public Information, New York, January 3, 1995.

Branaman, Brenda M., *Somalia: Chronology of Events, June 26, 1960–October 14, 1993,* Congressional Research Service, Washington, D.C., October 15, 1993.

Brooks, Geraldine, "Peacekeeping Missions of U.N. Are Pursued on a Wing and a Prayer," *Wall Street Journal,* December 28, 1993, p. 1.

Browne, Marjorie Ann, *United Nations Peacekeeping: Historical Overview,* Congressional Research Service, Washington, D.C., CRS Report 90-96F, January 31, 1990.

———, *United Nations Peacekeeping Operations 1988–1993: Background Information,* Congressional Research Service, Washington, D.C., CRS Report 94-193F, February 28, 1994.

Bruner, Edward F., *U.S. Forces and Multinational Commands: Precedents and Criteria,* Congressional Research Service, Washington, D.C., CRS Report 93-436F, April 21, 1993.

Cassesse, Antonio, ed., *United Nations Peacekeeping: Legal Essays,* Sijthoff and Noordhoff, Netherlands, 1978.

Copson, Raymond W., *Somalia: Operation Restore Hope,* Congressional Research Service, Washington, D.C., April 6, 1993.

Crocker, Chester A., "Peacekeeping We Can Fight For," *The Washington Post,* May 8, 1994, p. C1.

Dagne, Theodros S., *Somalia: A Country at War—Prospects for Peace and Reconciliation,* Congressional Research Service, Washington, D.C., June 15, 1992.

Diehl, Paul F., "Peacekeeping Operations and the Quest for Peace," *Political Science Quarterly,* Vol. 103, No. 3, 1988, pp. 485–507.

Durch, William J., ed., *The Evolution of UN Peacekeeping: Case Studies and Comparative Analysis,* St. Martin's Press, New York, 1993.

Dworken, Jonathan T., *Military Relations with Humanitarian Relief Organizations: Observations from Restore Hope*, Center for Naval Analyses, Alexandria, Va., CRM-94-140, October 1993.

Elganzoury, Abdelazim, *Evolution of the Peace Keeping Powers of the General Assembly of the United Nations*, General Egyptian Book Organization, Cairo, 1978.

Foss, John, et al., "U.S. Forces on the Golan Heights?" Center for Security Policy, Washington, D.C., October 25, 1994; reprinted in *Commentary*, December 1994.

Freeman, Waldo D., Robert B. Lambert, and Jason D. Mims, "Operation Restore Hope: A USCENTCOM Perspective," *Military Review*, September 1993.

Garvey, Jack, "United Nations Peacekeeping and Host State Consent," *American Journal of International Law*, April 1970, pp. 241–269.

Glenny, Misja, *The Fall of Yugoslavia: The Third Balkan War*, Penguin Books, New York, 1992.

Gonin, Jean-Marc, "ONU: Les Gardiens de la Paix," *L'Express*, April 15, 1993, pp. 20–25.

Gordenker, Leon, *Soldiers, Peacekeepers and Disasters*, St. Martin's Press, New York, 1991.

Herzog, Chaim, *The Arab-Israeli Wars*, Random House, New York, 1982.

Hoar, Joseph P., "A CINC's Perspective," *JFQ Forum*, Autumn 1993.

Joint Chiefs of Staff, *Unified Action Armed Forces (UNAAF)*, Washington, D.C., JCS Publication 0-2, December 1, 1986.

Kassebaum, Nancy L., and Lee H. Hamilton, *Peacekeeping and the US National Interest*, The Henry L. Stimson Center, Washington, D.C., Report No. 11, February 1994.

Kassing, David, *Transporting the Army for Operation Restore Hope*, RAND, Santa Monica, Calif., MR-384-A, 1994.

Lake, Anthony, "The Limits of Peacekeeping," *The New York Times,* February 6, 1994, p. D17.

Leibstone, Marvin, "Peacekeeping '94:   More Questions Than Answers," *Military Technology,* December 1994, pp. 84–85.

Lippman, Thomas W., "Use of U.S. Troops on Golan Heights Debated," *The Washington Post,* December 4, 1994, p. 42.

Lowenthal, Mark M., *Peacekeeping in Future U.S. Foreign Policy: CRS Report to Congress,* Congressional Research Service, Washington, D.C., March 21, 1994, pp. 1–22.

MacKenzie, Lewis, *Peacekeeper: The Road to Sarajevo,* Douglas & McIntyre, Vancouver, Canada, 1993.

Mann, Edward, "Military Support for 'Peace Efforts'," *Airpower Journal,* Fall 1993, pp. 51–56.

Merryman, James L., "New World Order Is Tested by Somalia," *The Christian Science Monitor,* February 1, 1995.

Nelson, Richard, "Multinational Peacekeeping in the Middle East and the United Nations Model," *International Affairs,* Winter 1984–85, pp. 67–89.

Rifkind, Malcolm, "Peacekeeping or Peacemaking? Implications and Prospects," *RUSI Journal,* April 1993, pp. 1–6.

Rikhye, Indar Jit, Michael Harbottle, and Bjorn Egge, *The Thin Blue Line: International Peacekeeping and Its Future,* Yale University Press, New Haven, Conn., 1974.

Roberts, Adam, "The Crisis in UN Peacekeeping," *Survival, The IISS Quarterly,* Autumn 1994, pp. 93–120.

Roos, John G., "The Perils of Peacekeeping: Tallying the Costs in Blood, Coin, Prestige, and Readiness," *Armed Forces Journal International,* December 1993, pp. 13–17.

Saksena, K. P., "Not by Design: Evolution of U.N. Peacekeeping Operations and Its Implications for the Future," *International Studies,* October–December 1977, pp. 459–481.

Sherry, George L., *The United Nations: Conflict Control in the Post–Cold War World*, Council on Foreign Relations, New York, 1990.

Siegel, Adam B., *Requirements for Humanitarian Assistance and Peace Operations: Insights from Seven Case Studies*, Center for Naval Analyses, Alexandria, Va., CRM-94-74, March 1995.

Sloan, Stanley R., *Peacekeeping and Conflict Management Activities: A Discussion of Terms*, Congressional Research Service, Washington, D.C., CRS Report 93-1017S, November 26, 1993.

Swift, Richard, "United Nations Military Training for Peace," *International Organization*, Spring 1974, pp. 267–280.

Tharoor, Shashi, "Peacekeeping: Principles, Problems, Prospects," *Naval War College Review*, Spring 1994, pp. 9–22.

United Nations, *Agenda for Peace—1992* [see United Nations, *Preventive Diplomacy*, for full citation].

——, *The Blue Helmets: A Review of United Nations Peace-Keeping*, Department of Public Information, New York, 1990.

——, *Charter of the United Nations*, San Francisco, Calif., June 25, 1945.

——, *Preventive Diplomacy, Peacemaking and Peace-Keeping: Report of the Secretary-General Pursuant to the Statement Adopted by the Summit Meeting of the Security Council on 31 January 1992*, A/47/277, S/24111, New York, June 17, 1992; short title: *Agenda for Peace—1992*.

——, *Supplement to An Agenda for Peace: Position Paper of the Secretary-General on the Occasion of the Fiftieth Anniversary of the United Nations*, A/50/60, S/1995/1, New York, January 3, 1995; short title: *Agenda for Peace—1995*.

——, *The United Nations and Cambodia 1991–1995*, Department of Public Information, New York, 1995.

——, *United Nations Peace-keeping*, Department of Public Information, New York, August 1993.

————, *Universal Declaration of Human Rights*, adopted by General Assembly on 10 December 1948.

"United Nations Peacekeeping Operations: History, Resources, Missions, and Components," *International Defense Review: Defense 1995*, 1995, pp. 119–127.

U.S. Department of State, *The Clinton Administration's Policy on Reforming Multilateral Peace Operations*, Washington, D.C., Publication 10161, May 1994.

U.S. Department of the Army, Center for Lessons Learned, United States Army Combined Arms Command, *Operation Restore Hope: Operations Other Than War*, Fort Leavenworth, Kansas, August 16, 1993.

————, Headquarters, 1st Brigade, 10th Mountain Division (Light Infantry), *After Action Report: Task Force Mountain Warrior*, Fort Drum, New York, September 30, 1993.

————, 10th Mountain Division (LI), U.S. Army Forces, Somalia, *After Action Report*, Fort Drum, New York, June 2, 1993.

U.S. General Accounting Office, National Security and International Affairs Division, *Humanitarian Intervention: Effectiveness of U.N. Operations in Bosnia*, Washington, D.C., GAO/NSIAD-94-156BR, April 1994.

————, National Security and International Affairs Division, *U.N. Peacekeeping: Lessons Learned in Managing Recent Missions*, GAO/NSIAD-94-9, December 1993.

————, National Security and International Affairs Division, *United Nations: U.S. Participation in Peacekeeping Operations*, Washington, D.C., GAO/NSIAD-92-247, September 1992.

U.S. Government, *A National Security Strategy of Engagement and Enlargement*, The White House, Washington, D.C., July 1994.

U.S. Institute of Peace, *Contributions to the Study of Peacemaking, Volume 3*, Washington, D.C., 1993.

Van Heuven, Marten, "Rehabilitating Serbia," *Foreign Policy*, Fall 1994, pp. 38–56.

Von Koispoth, Edward, "Airborne Surveillance for U.N. Crisis Management," *Military Technology*, December 1994, pp. 87–88.

Ward, Don, "Getting a Handle on Peacekeeping," *Navy Times*, March 14, 1994, p. 29.

Warrington, Robert D., "The Helmets May Be Blue, but the Blood's Still Red: The Dilemma of U.S. Participation in U.N. Peace Operations," *Comparative Strategy*, Vol. 14, No. 1, 1995, pp. 23–34.

Zimmerman, Warren, "The Last Ambassador: A Memoir of the Collapse of Yugoslavia," *Foreign Affairs*, March/April 1995, pp. 2–20.

JX 1981 .P7 P56 1996 c.1
Pirnie, Bruce, 1940-
Soldiers for peace

DATE DUE

GAYLORD   PRINTED IN U.S.A.